THE COMPLETE BOOK OF
EVERLASTINGS

*Growing, Drying,
and Designing with
Dried Flowers*

Mark and Terry Silber

ALFRED A. KNOPF
NEW YORK 1988

THIS IS A BORZOI BOOK
PUBLISHED BY ALFRED A. KNOPF, INC.

Library of Congress Cataloging-in-Publication Data
Silber, Mark.
The Complete Book of Everlastings:
Growing, Drying, and Designing with Dried Flowers.
1. Everlasting flowers. 2. Flower gardening.
3. Flowers—drying. 4. Dried flower arrangement.
I. Silber, Terry, [date]. II. Title.
SB428.5.S55 1987 745.92 87-45121
ISBN 0-394-74370-9
Manufactured in the United States of America
First Paperback Edition

The text of this book was set in Caslon 540.
Composed by American-Stratford Graphic
Service, Inc., Brattleboro, Vermont.
Printed and bound by Bookbuilders Ltd.,
Hong Kong

DESIGNED BY JULIE DUQUET
ASSISTED BY LINDA SARRO

This book is dedicated to
Bernard and Marion Tripp,
who have enthusiastically and tirelessly
supported our flowering endeavors.

Contents

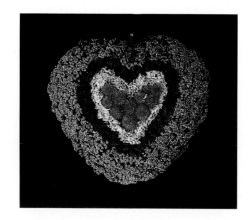

Acknowledgments

Many people have contributed to the production of this book. Seeding, transplanting, weeding and collecting flowers require physical stamina, perseverance and a good sense of humor. Over the years, Pamela Chodosh, Phyllis Corson, Roger Crockett, Christopher Drouin, Michael Dudek, Philip Dyer, Diego Erausquin, Anne Siekman, Bernard Tripp and Elzibeth Volk have set a pace for getting the job done carefully and intelligently. We are further indebted to Teri Gordon, Eiko Fulenwider, Cathy Lee, Carolee Newton and Marion Tripp for their creative abilities in designing with everlastings. Librarians at the Gray Herbarium and Widener Library at Harvard University, the Library of Congress in Washington, D.C., as well as those at Bates College in Lewiston, Maine, were helpful in directing us to some elusive sources of information. David Emery of Wolf's Neck Farm, Freeport, Maine, is responsible for the design of the heather and heath gardens. Mariette R. Hebert of Morin's Bridal World has generously given her time and studio for photographing the wedding products. Richard Folsom of the Maine Department of Agriculture has assisted us in identifying a number of insect species. Dr. Horacio Lichter was hospitable in inviting us to photograph some arrangements in his home. We would also like to thank our editor, Jane Garrett, for her support, her helpful comments and her belief in this project.

THE COMPLETE BOOK OF

EVERLASTINGS

1
Introduction

Everlastings, immortelles or dry flowers are all names used interchangeably for that unique category of plants that retain their color and shape long after they have been picked and dried. They are available in a broad variety of colors, from the subtle tones of common yarrows to the intense and vibrant purples of statice and the brilliant magentas of cockscomb. While many of the flowers are daisy-shaped, there are also some that are spikes, plumes and clusters of button-like blooms. Grasses, leaves and pods are also included in this category of plants.

The majority of these everlastings differ from other flowers in that, even when they are alive, they possess very little moisture and thus feel almost papery to the touch. Given the wonderful variety of plants that are suitable for drying, it is no wonder that, over the ages, people have had various uses and meanings for these materials.

The everlastings that we will focus on in this book will be those that can be dried simply by hanging. There are more complex methods for removing the moisture from many flowers, but when we refer to the immortelles, we are talking about those plant forms that can be gathered and dried by hanging. For successful results, you will come to see, one needs to understand the botany of each variety and, with that, to know the proper time to gather so that its color and form will remain attractive and durable for handling.

Found throughout the temperate and tropical zones, everlastings traveled with their admirers. From mid-Asia, from Australia, from Africa and the Americas, conquerors, colonists and travelers have distributed seeds and plants throughout the world. In many cultures, everlastings not only were used to decorate homes, they were also incorporated into elaborate cultural rituals. Unlike cut flowers, which were but short-lived or unavailable during certain seasons, everlastings maintained their beauty for years. While cut flowers came to symbolize beauty and fleeting life, everlastings represented longevity and immortality. Thus, everlastings came to symbolize long life and power—even after death.

Wreaths and garlands, from both cut and dried flowers, were hung on walls and columns, placed on tables and pedestals, worn on heads and draped on shoulders. The use of wreaths made of fresh or dry flowers can be traced back to the first solar myths of civilization. As a social symbol, a wreath symbolized achievement and honor. As a circular object, a wreath represented continuity, in both theological and biological terms. Crowns and halos bedecked the heads of important people such as kings and saints, heroes and magistrates, virgins and sacrificial victims.

Before cut flowers were available year-round, everlastings were the only alternative

long-lasting flowers. They were desirable because their form and color were always a reminder of nature's beauty. Everlastings are, however, not forever-lasting. Depending on the amount of ambient humidity and light, some everlastings may stay beautiful for months, others for years. But eventually, unless everlastings are in total darkness and a controlled environment, their color will fade, their fragrance will dissipate and their structural integrity will succumb to the stresses of climate changes. Over time, as with all natural color and fiber, everlastings will deteriorate.

During the Victorian era, people sought to prolong the life of everlastings by placing small arrangements in bell jars. But in that era of great experimentation, people also began to fabricate flowers and plants out of other materials, such as wool and waxed paper. At the turn of the century, glass beads came into vogue. Then, with the widespread use of plastics during World War II, the floral industry gave us a variety of plant material that was inexpensive, washable and quite colorful. While we may argue the merits of artificial flowers, they made their way into a worldwide market and had a significant effect on the use of real dried materials for a number of years.

In the continuing search for long-lasting plant material, manufacturers offered us silk and polyester flowers. These various materials have their own desirable and undesirable features. Silk has a texture that is most like the real flower, but it fades and, like dried flowers, cannot be washed because it loses shape and color. The less expensive polyester has an undesirable sheen, but you can wash it, you can deform it and it springs back. These materials quite effectively reproduced natural flowers, but human creativity did not stop with the attempt to duplicate nature. Soon flowers were made up to emulate rather than replicate real flowers. They were enlarged and reduced. Whimsically, characteristics of diverse flowers were joined together to produce plant-like forms.

For some, these artificial alternatives solve many problems with decoration. For others, there is no alternative to real flowers, whether fresh or everlasting. With all their detriments, real flowers evoke stronger associations between nature and us. Writing in the 1950s, Alice Coats, an avid gardener and a flower historian, thought that the transition from the use of real flowers to the use of bead flowers represented the moral degradation of nature's sanctity. Her terse remark that real dried flowers "have been superseded . . . by atrocious flowers of no known species, made of beads strung on wire, about which the less said the better," spoke for many who saw in real flowers not only a decorative significance but also their own place in nature.

FLOWERS FROM THE DAWN OF HISTORY

Both fresh and everlasting flowers, as decoration and as symbol, are woven into the history of mankind. Early records do not refer specifically to everlastings in their discussion of flowers, and thus a look at the history of flower usage includes all varieties of flowers and plants. There is evidence to suggest that the use of flowers per se has been continuous with the development of civilization. The most obvious record of how different civilizations used flowers comes from the written description of events, festivals and celebrations. Yet a flower painted on a potsherd, a flower carved in marble, an impression of a flower shape on a coin are all tangibly suggestive of human interest in flowers. Some archaeological finds point to evidence that human beings were

Achillea millefolium var. *rosea*

interested in flowers even before the earliest written or pictorial material.

Perhaps the most important characteristic distinguishing humans from other members of the animal kingdom is the development of culture—the human ability to create symbols. Other animals use tools, other animals convey learned information, but human beings adapt their environment in a symbolic and ritual fashion. The use of symbols, it has been postulated, is the dividing line between "modern" man and his ancestors.

Until as late as the last decade, anthropologists, paleontologists and other scientists did not believe that Neanderthals should be regarded as modern humans because, although they left behind manufactured tools, they did not leave any artifacts that could be interpreted as indicators of culture. Then, in some very unexpected and exciting excavations in northern Iraq in the mid-1970s, a team of archaeologists and palynologists discovered a burial site in a Shanidar cave. It was not a chance deposition of human bones. There were, among the remains, bones of a man, two women and a baby. They were dated as 60,000 years old.

It was a significant find, not only because the bodies were laid out in an orderly fashion—suggestive of a rudimentary funeral (a distinct example of cultural behavior)—but also because the microscopic evidence suggested that the burial was ritual in nature. The palynologists discovered that, with the bones, there was pollen of flowers common in that region to the present day. Flowers, more than any of the other material items found in archaeological digs of that age, tell us that these people may have had what some anthropologists refer to as "soul"—an ability to create and use natural objects as cultural or social abstractions. Using flowers in death, these prehistoric Neanderthal beings had commemorated their existence in what may be the earliest record of human ritual activity.

The kinds of flowers found support this notion, particularly because they could not have made their way into the cave accidentally. Collected over a large territory, these flowers must have been made into bouquets and deposited on the "grave." Included there were species of plants that have been valued by later peoples for medicinal uses (and some are now used as dry flowers). Among them were *Achillea* (yarrow), *Centaurea cyanus* (bachelor's button); *Centaurea solstitialis* (St. Barnaby's thistle), various species of *Senecio* (some are cultivated in our gardens as dusty miller), *Muscari* (grape hyacinth), *Alcea rosea* (hollyhock) and others.

The presence of flowers also suggested that those who were buried at the cave were of a high social status. The notion that social status is associated with flowers is also conveyed through pictorial records from Egypt as early as 3000 B.C. Gardens of flowers and exotic plants have been the property of kings, emperors and powerful notables. Gardens for pleasure and delight, as opposed to gardens fulfilling basic human needs for food, have been associated with the highest echelons of society. The mythological gardens of Hesperides, *oz peri*, fruit gardens (according to some scholars, situated in Africa); the gardens of Alcinoüs, a Phaeacian king; and even the Garden of Eden are associated with concepts of power. Oriental cultures—Japanese and Chinese, for example—have developed gardens and designs with flowers into a high art form. And even the ideas of Heaven and Paradise as gardens permeate the eschatology of many of the world's great religions—Judaism, Christianity, Islam and Hinduism.

FLOWERS IN ANCIENT EGYPT, GREECE AND ROME

The Egyptian queen Hatshepsut and her brother Thutmose III (c. 1500–1450 B.C.) were the first to import exotic and rare plants from Africa and Asia specifically for the pleasure that they provided. Egyptians were also known for their lavish use of flowers. Engraved pictures show profuse offerings of flowers for the entombed souls. Pharaohs ostentatiously displayed floral bounty. It is recorded that Ramses III (c. 1230 B.C.) for his feasts ordered 3,100 tall bouquets, 19,150 large bouquets, 12,400 blue

flowers in ropes, 153,600 garlands, 110 flower strings, 46,500 flowers to hold, 3,410 lotus-flower bouquets, 3,261,604 bouquets of blossoms and 3,125,800 measures of blossoms. Papyrus stems, papyrus flowers, herbs, berries and other plant materials were also popular.

There is ample evidence that flowers were used in social rituals. Funeral garlands found in coffins contained elaborate flower ornaments fashioned with date-leaf fiber. In the coffin of King Ahmes I (c. 1700 B.C.) there were small wreaths made with blue delphiniums, still colorful when found 3,000 years later. In the coffin of Princess Nesi-Khonsu (c. 1000 B.C.) a garland contained willow leaves and poppy petals. Among the everlasting flowers that we recognize in Egyptian records are *Helichrysum arenarium* and *Delphinium* species, which were used in wreaths to symbolize immortality.

In the homes of Egyptian notables it was customary to entertain guests in an environment permeated with the fragrance of flowers. Hosts, holding lotus flowers in their hands, were seated in a double chair. As guests arrived, they were presented with lotus flowers to hold in their hands. Servants hung garlands on guests and anointed their heads with sweetly scented ointments. Guests and servants alike wore wreaths of fresh flowers.

The extensive use of flowers, herbs and decorative plants in ancient Greece is commemorated in the myths and legends of gods and heroes. Plants were said to be sacred to various gods and goddesses. Greeks associated the oak and the pinks with Jupiter (Druids, a thousand years later, ascribed to the oak supernatural powers); the pomegranate, iris and lily with Hera; the apple, myrtle and rose with Aphrodite; the poppy with Demeter and Artemis. Beautiful flowers were also thought to have been created by gods and goddesses from the blood or bodies of Greek heroes. Venus, who was passionately in love with Adonis, immortalized her dead lover by creating the short-lived anemone (windflower) from his blood. Apollo, fond of the youth Hyacinthus, created a blue flower called hyacinth when Hyacinthus was tragically killed during a game. All of us are familiar with the story of

Narcissus from our study of mythology in elementary school. Narcissus was a beautiful young man. For his cruelty to the fragile nymph Echo, he was punished and was turned into a pale flower.

According to the Greek historian Themistagoras, the name *Helichrysum* was derived from the name of the nymph Elichrysa, who used it to adorn the goddess Artemis. John Gerard, a sixteenth-century English herbalist, writes: "For which cause of long lasting the images and carved gods were wont to weare garlands thereof: whereupon some have called it 'God's floure.' For which purpose Ptolemy, king of Aegypt, did most diligently observe them, as Pliny writeth."

The Greeks revered nature and it was the Greeks who first undertook a major exploration and recording of plants in their environment. The work of the Greek botanist Theophrastus (d. 287 B.C.), who wrote a major study of the history of plants, was the basic text of the science of botany for two thousand years—until the passing of the Dark Ages. In his manuscript, he discussed horticultural methods of propagation and forcing, common names in various geographic areas and the medicinal uses of plants.

Greeks celebrated various plants because they were preoccupied with the significance and aesthetics of their environment. Learned men such as Thales of Miletus (c. 636–546 B.C.) and his pupil Anaximander were the first in recorded history to postulate non-theological origins of the world. Xenophanes of Colophon (c. 570–475 B.C.) and Herodotus (c. 484–425 B.C.) were the first to recognize differences in human societies and to list various cultural items such as customs, languages, religions and laws, as well as material culture, including such objects as flowers used in rituals and social functions.

Thus, ancient Greeks used plants symbolically. Plants commemorated their loved ones in life and in death. A wild-olive crown was awarded to a victor in the Olympic Games, crowns of laurel and palm were awarded in the Pythian games and crowns of parsley in the Nemean. Greeks used *Gomphrena globosa* (globe amaranth) and perhaps *Amaranthus caudatus* to shower the body of slain Achilles to betoken his immortality.

Gomphrena globosa in the foreground, *Ageratum houstonii* mixed with *Eucalyptus cinerea* at right.

The bodies of other fallen heroes were similarly strewn with amaranths and other everlasting plants symbolic of remembrance.

Incorporating nature's beauty into their social fabric, the Greeks developed an elaborate system of designating social status with flowers and herbs. Status was indicated by the kinds of flowers used in crowns. Coronary plants used during Theophrastus' time include: asphodel, Attic thyme, bergamot mint, *Dianthus*, *Helichrysum*, iris, rose, lavender, violet, spirea, southernwood, parsley and myrtle. Myrtle was so favored that flower markets came to be known as myrtle markets and various wreaths were made to be readily available when the demand increased.

The Romans adapted many Greek customs and beliefs to their own culture. Their use of flowers and herbs as signs of social status paralleled that of the Greeks. For them, using crowns was akin to our use of medals. A *corona obsidionalis*, consisting of grasses or wildflowers, was

worn by generals who were instrumental in forcing an enemy to raise siege. A *corona triumphalis*, consisting of laurel and bay leaves, was worn by victorious generals. Myrtle made up a *corona ovalis* but was awarded to commanders of lesser distinction. Various other crowns were worn daily or on special occasions. *Hibernae coronae* were made of dried flowers. The *corona sutiles* was made of flowers and leaves.

Since each crown had a specific symbolic meaning, the use of improper plants in crowns was severely punished. A well-publicized case concerns L. Fulvius, a powerful general during the Second Punic War (the famous Hannibal war), 218–201 B.C. Shortly after the war started, Fulvius was accused of wearing a crown of roses in public. But crowns of roses were regal. Mercilessly, the Roman Senate imprisoned him for the duration of the war—for seventeen years. Cicero prosecuted Verres, a Roman governor of Sicily, for similar transgressions.

In family life and in entertaining, the Romans were also liberal in their use of flower material for decoration. During the early years of the Roman Empire, it was customary to wear simple wreaths and garlands. But the variety and ostentation increased with conquests and amassed wealth. Roman notables competed to be acknowledged by their peers for the lavishness of their floral decor. This fever reached tragicomic proportions when Heliogabalus (a fourteen-year-old Syrian who was proclaimed Emperor of Rome in A.D. 218) ordered his servants to shower guests with such a volume of rose petals that several people suffocated in the abundance.

THE EARLY AND MIDDLE CHRISTIAN PERIOD

The historical record of how the early Christians used flowers is unclear. On the one hand, the early Christians, in contrasting their own religious ritual to that of the Romans, apparently rejected the use of garlands, wreaths and other such material as adornment. On the other hand, there is ample evidence that animals, fish, birds, flowers and plants were employed to symbolize various aspects of Christianity. For example, St. Bernard writes about the Annunciation: "The flower willed to be born of a flower, in a flower, at the time of flowers." This statement, it is suggested, was instrumental in a later development of the lily as a symbol of purity.

As time passed and the immediate threat of comparison between Christian monotheism and Roman polytheism diminished, Christians wove the old Greek and Roman legends into their symbolism by associating representational flowers with their own saints. The lily, Venus' flower, became the Virgin's flower. The amaranths, including globe amaranth, which was woven by Greeks into garlands, came to represent the immortality of Jesus. Amaranths decorated the altars of Portuguese churches. However, flowers were not used by Christians as ostentatiously or as lavishly as they were used before the diffusion of Christianity.

During the Middle Ages, Christians concentrated on the more utilitarian characteristics of

Papaver rhoe

Helichrysum thianschanicum

flowers and herbs, primarily their medicinal uses. Consistently, herbals of the period listed plants by categories of curative "virtues." If virtues were unknown, plants were categorized as those whose virtues were yet to be discovered. Many plants were assigned omnipotent properties. *Potentilla*, for instance, gets its botanical name from such an association. Comfrey, a common herb in every garden, had similar connotations.

But other plants came to be associated with evil. Among these was the common thistle, whose sharp thorns were said to be the work of the devil. Rue and vervain, prominent in Greek society as symbolic of ill fate, were seen by some Christians as plants of witchcraft. Others were supposed to ward off the effects of the Evil Eye. Artemisia was used as a witch repellent and as a moth repellent. The incorporation of plants into European Christian beliefs and lore paralleled their use as remedies of one sort or another.

A PERIOD OF DISCOVERY

With the passing of the Middle Ages, interest in plants for their beauty rather than for their medicinal uses was on the upswing. Western Europeans started to explore distant lands. Like their ancient predecessors, explorers sought new plants and new flowers. These adventurers were inquisitive but many also sought to profit from their discoveries by introducing the public to new plants for food and decoration. New plants were acquired from the Americas, Asia and Australia. Potatoes, tomatoes and corn are the best-known New World introductions. But others— *Ageratum* from the American tropics, *Clematis* and *Tradescantia* from the region of Virginia and *Anaphalis* (pearly everlasting) from Acadia—also became popular.

The interest in these new flowers quickly permeated the Continent. When Gerard assembled his herbal at the end of the sixteenth century, he was almost apologetic upon encountering a flower such as *Aquilegia*, which had no virtues. Columbine, its common name, was not known for any particular healing properties. But

by the eighteenth century, English nurserymen published catalogues that listed various flowers for the garden and home, and everlastings formed a separate category among them.

Toward the end of the eighteenth century, from Australia, such everlastings as *Helichrysum bracteatum* (strawflower), *Helipterum roseum* (acroclinium), *Helipterum humboltianum* and *Helipterum manglesii* (rhodanthe) were introduced into England and shortly thereafter into North America. By the early nineteenth century Thomas Jefferson's garden walks were lined with globe amaranth, later to be used in winter bouquets.

Although everlasting flowers were used for decoration inside homes much earlier, by the end of the nineteenth century that interest increased tremendously, judging by garden catalogue offerings of the day. In the United States, the 1891 Eastman's Annual Seed Catalogue from East Sumner, Maine, offered acroclinium, *Ammobium*, *Gomphrena*, *Helichrysum* and *Xeranthemum*. In the 1886 Johnson and Stokes Farm Manual, published in Philadelphia, listings included the same varieties as Eastman along with such ornamental grasses as *Eulalia japonica*, *Agrostis*, *Coix* (Job's tears), *Lagurus* and pampas, and an unusual flower, rhodanthe. In the same year, Storrs & Harrison Co. from Painesville, Ohio, offered *Helipterum anthemoides*, a plant not prominent in any contemporary American seed catalogue.

Mid-eighteenth-century American settlers in Virginia adapted the formal English gardens to their new environment. Gardens, though less formal, were an important part of the home. Gardening, specifically with flowers and herbs, was a woman's occupation and the young women were trained as much in the art of design with "artificial flowers" as they were to do embroidery, play musical instruments and dance. The *Virginia Gazette* dated March 21, 1766, for example, carried an advertisement by E. Gardner, who had a school where young ladies of refined taste would be taught "embroidery, queenstitch, shading, Dresden lace work . . . and artificial flowers."

In part, the interest in growing flowers for their beauty was brought on by the period of discovery and the introduction of new plants into the standard European repertoire. In part, the interest in flowers was buoyed because of their symbolic meanings. Flowers, as already noted, have been associated with magic and ritual. But not until Lady Mary Wortley Montagu, wife of the British ambassador to the Turkish sultan in Constantinople in the early 1720s, returned to England with a list of "exact" meanings for flowers did flowers become for Europeans a medium of human communication. Influenced by her Oriental acquaintances, she suggested that flowers had specific meanings to express passion, friendship, agreement and altercation. The specific floral meanings were later gathered and published (approximately 1840) in a book, *Le Langage des Fleurs,* by Madame de la Tour in France. The language of flowers developed into a Victorian cult. For some, the previously accepted method of communication—writing—became less interesting, replaced temporarily by intricate assemblages of flowers to convey messages.

Depending on how the flowers were presented, where they were worn, at what stage in their flowering they were utilized, what their predominant color theme was, certain ideas were communicated. If a marigold was placed in the hair, it could mean "sorrow of the mind." If it was placed on the breast, it could mean "boredom." If it was placed on the heart, it could mean "pangs of love." According to Claire Powell, the Adonis flower meant sorrowful remembrances; agrimony, thankfulness; narcissus, egoism or self-esteem; peppermint, cordiality; gathered flowers, we die together. These romantic notions and the means of communicating them through flowers appealed to people in the late nineteenth century. It was a turbulent period when war, industrialization and social stratifica-

tion gave rise to philosophical discourses as to the nature of mankind. Romantics drew on the philosophies of Rousseau (1712–1778) and Herder (1744–1803) to glorify man's preliterate or "primitive" past. Studies of mythology and folklore became academic disciplines, and Charles Darwin (1809–1882) presented his theory of evolution.

Perhaps it is to be expected that, during this period when people were more sensitive to the relationship between environment and human beings, the interest in flowers, plants and animals would again become not only socially acceptable but ultimately desirable. From the philosophers to the uneducated people, everyone strove to be romantically enticed by nature. In this cultural climate, an American turn-of-the-century treatise on etiquette, dress, beauty and domestic relations entitled *Social Culture* intoned that, in order to achieve social perfection, one had to grow and live with plants. From this experience one was "to gain an appreciation of the beautiful in distinction from the sublime and grand, to secure a refined and correct taste and to learn to enjoy harmony of colors, delicacy of form and beauty of outline . . ."

This language is archaic and the purpose for growing plants is not the same as ours, but our feelings about plants, animals and wildlife are remarkably similar. Now, as people did in the past, we reflect on our place in nature. We take care to preserve the environment and to take pleasure in its survival—for us and for future generations. We are sensitive to the interdependence between us and everything that surrounds us. When we grow flowers, we reap the satisfaction of having a hand in creating something that is beautiful. When we work with real flowers, we are also aware of the history and the philosophies that those flowers represent.

2

From Seed to Harvest

For the past two decades or so, there has been an increased awareness of the interest in flowers for drying. As a result, not only are there everlastings imported on a large scale from Holland, Australia and other countries, but there are many commercial growers who have included everlastings in their field crops. Thus, the availability of dried flowers has grown to the point where you can buy bunches from florists, craft stores, garden club sales, flea markets and farmers' markets across the country. For those of you interested in working with everlastings, it is not necessary to produce all of your own raw materials. And if you are without garden space or the ability to gather in the wild, there is still the possibility of purchasing and designing with everlastings. But many of you will feel that there is no substitute for everlastings that you grow yourself. You reap rewards not only of higher quality and greater variety but also of the pleasure in designing with flowers that you intimately know.

If you decide to grow your own plants, you should know that in order to achieve a high yield in a short-season climate, all everlastings should be started indoors, either early in the spring or late in the winter. As an alternative, you can purchase your seedlings in the spring. You may be tempted to seed outdoors. No doubt you can germinate certain hardy perennials. You may even be able to grow some hardy annuals in coldframes. It is unlikely, however, that you will find this satisfying, for plants that are started inside produce crops earlier, produce them faster and produce for a longer period of time because they do not have to fight weeds, highly fluctuating temperatures and fungi that proliferate in cool spring soils. Also, rare, unusual, or fine-seeded plants should have special treatment even in a warmer climate. For these reasons, all our seeds are started indoors.

Plants that are started in an indoor environment thrive because they have near ideal conditions. They get constant moisture, heat, light and food. Plants in nature rarely have an ideal combination of factors for growth. Because we want the greatest possible number of our plants to do well, we manage their environment.

In nature, a plant produces numerous seeds, only a portion of which survive. In a controlled environment, the odds are greatly increased. What we can accomplish is nothing short of a miracle—a high rate of germination, a high rate of survival and a uniformity that is not found in nature. Plants from near and far thrive under these controlled conditions. For example, *Helichrysum* from Australia, *Limonium* from Southern Europe, *Gomphrena* from India and *Agastache* from North America all perform well in the same greenhouse or even under lights.

A garden of everlastings starts with careful planning. Plants are seeded, transplanted, set out in the garden, maintained, harvested and dried. The process of growing and designing with everlastings is characterized by pleasure and satisfaction of accomplishment, not only with the wreath or arrangement that adorns your home but also with the fact that you have intimately known, cared for and worked with the plant that produced the flowers. The discipline, care and inevitable involvement result in flowers of beauty and fragrance and textures that last long after the snows have fallen.

This chapter contains pointers and shortcuts that will help you get started in raising plants of your own. If you purchase plants, skip over the parts that deal with seeding. If you plan to pick only in the wild, read the section on harvesting, for there are some rules that apply to picking, bunching, hanging and drying all kinds of flowers, both cultivated and wild.

PURCHASING SEED

Seed Catalogues

The process of growing plants from seeds often starts with purchasing seeds from catalogues published by seed companies. Every winter we curl up with a dozen seed catalogues from the United States, Great Britain and Canada, to determine which seeds we will plant in the spring. Some seed catalogues are large and glamorous with hundreds of full-color illustrations; others are mere sheets of duplicated paper, enumerating their offerings of the season. Whether printed on glossy stock or on newsprint, catalogues provide a wealth of information, not only because they list and illustrate plants but also because they are guides to germination and cultivation, relative sizes and seasonal hardiness of plants.

Catalogues are organized differently. One may offer information about the time that is required to grow a plant from seed to bloom, while another may be more concerned with origins and the size of the plant. The catalogues that we appreciate are to the point. They use botanical names, so that we know exactly which plant we are purchasing. They have information about the time required for germination, so that we can plan our seeding schedule. They give data about quantities of seed in a packet and per unit of weight. This allows us to decide how many seeds we must purchase in order to grow a specific number of plants. Some catalogues also note germination rates—what proportion of the seeds is expected to be viable. In any catalogue, a certain style or type of data may appeal to one person but not another. These differences and similarities allow us to compare information and facilitate the making of intelligent decisions.

A word about plants and plant names. In their catalogues many reputable seed companies use, in addition to common names, botanical names. Do not be afraid of them. You certainly can deal with names like *Petunia* and *Calendula*, which are botanical names. Linnaeus, a Swedish botanist who lived in the eighteenth century, developed a system of scientific (binomial) names. He standardized relationships of plants by assigning them names based on the taxonomy of their reproductive organs (in the case of flowering plants, flowers are reproductive organs). These names are useful not only because they substitute for the many common regional names but also because they emphasize how one plant is related to another.

For instance, common florist's statice is *Limonium sinuata*. The first name is the genus name; the second is the species name. With a binomial name, we can tell that *Limonium carolinianum*, known as sea lavender, sea heather or marsh rosemary (it is neither a lavender, a heather nor a rosemary), is related to *Limonium sinuata*. These two plants belong to a more encompassing category of related plants. Specifically, the Plumbaginaceae family (named after the genus of another member of the family, *Plumbago*) also contains *Armeria maritima*, thrift.

Why would you want to use botanical names instead of the common names that you know? Botanical names are exact. Botanical names are cross-cultural. Only one scientific name is acceptable per plant. This is in a marked contrast to common names. There are many common names for plants depending on the country, the region or the history of the area. Common names are

Whether on glossy stock or newsprint, seed and nursery catalogues provide a wealth of horticultural information.

confusing because they may refer to different plants. For instance, there are at least six unrelated plants that are called dusty miller because of their gray foliage. What is even more important is that some plants do not even have common English names. If you plan to grow a plant, you must know what to expect. Would it not be better to get the plant that you expect to get? The only way to assure this is to use botanical names. At first, it is like learning another language, but later it becomes second nature.

Decisions about the purchase of seeds should be made at least three months before one expects to start seeding, for high demand may create shortages for a particular seed house. Building in a cushion of time allows for backup ordering of seed from other catalogues. It is important to know exactly what you are ordering and to let seed companies know whether they can substitute for a similar species or variety without consulting you. It is also important to consider the fact that many seed companies must design catalogues a year in advance. They have to depend on an irregular market supply and the vagaries of weather (some seeds never get harvested). Knowledge of these possible problems and planning ahead can save much time and annoyance.

Seeds from the largest seed companies now come in sophisticated packages that are made of either aluminum or plastic-lined paper. These packages are hermetically sealed to maintain constant humidity and to sustain a seed in storage for a long period of time. Packages from smaller companies may be hand-filled and come in small paper envelopes. However, the advantage of these small companies is that they offer rare seeds that may not be feasible for a large commercial company to stock.

Seed packages may also contain germination rates (such as 80 percent—meaning that 80 percent of the seeds are expected to germinate); others may have the date of harvest and still others may have the country of origin. If seeds are bought from a garden center, packets may also contain general and specific seeding information—if the seeds are to be started indoors or outdoors, how far apart and how deeply they should be planted, how the plants should be thinned.

The packages contain seeds big and small depending on the kind of plant from which they come. Within a species, different varieties may be of different sizes. And even within varieties some seeds will be larger and some will be smaller. The variation also depends on the specimen from which the seed has been harvested. In part, this variation depends on genetic inheritance. In a mixture of seeds of one species, it is not at all unusual to find a variation in size of seeds. In a species which has different colors—*Gomphrena*, globe amaranth, for example—color may be associated with a germination rate. Thus, you would be well advised to keep all germinated seedlings if you suspect that there will be variation. In fact, some surprises may be in store

Seeds may come in sophisticated packages made of aluminum or plastic-lined paper. Smaller seed companies usually package in hand-filled paper envelopes.

These packages contain seeds big and small, depending on the plant from which they come.

because you may get most unusual colors from slower-growing and smaller seedlings.

When you are ready to order seeds you may be given certain options as to the types of seed you can choose. Generally, three types are available: raw seeds—seeds in their husks or flowers; clean or *decorticated* seeds—seeds without husks or similar covering; and pelleted seeds—fine seeds that are coated with a substance to make their individual bulk larger for easier handling and spacing during seeding. The least expensive are raw seeds. The most expensive are seeds that have been pelleted.

You should also be aware of the fact that many seed companies treat seeds with fungicides and/or insecticides. You can recognize these treated seeds by their dark pink or blue tinge. Seed companies may treat seeds to prevent deterioration in storage. In some cases, innate moisture of the seeds condenses inside packets and the seeds mildew. The chemical compounds that are used to treat seeds are poisonous. You are well advised not to use the seed for extracting oil or for consumption. Also, you should handle such seeds carefully.

SEEDING

In preparation for seeding, you should figure out the time it will take for a seed to germinate and reach the transplanting stage. Also, you should consider the final size of the plant when it is ready to be set out into the garden. Plants are best grown at a steady rate. Because space in a seeding container is limited, plants can grow only to a certain point without experiencing visible deterioration. When plants run out of room or nutrients, their production in the field will diminish. Plants that are seeded too early will become leggy—tall, with weak stems and leaves that are far apart. Plants that are seeded too late will be too small for the field. An ideal plant ready for the field will be approximately six inches tall. It should have a strong stem, a dark green color and fibrous leaves. To determine time of germination, approximate growth rates and any special treatment of seeds (such as

chilling or freezing, presence or absence of light), you should consult your seed catalogues.

Seeding is the first part of the process during which a plant is raised, in a controlled environment, to a stage where it is set out into the field. The second stage is *transplanting*. At the beginning of this stage, the plant will be approximately one to two inches tall and will have developed some true leaves. The last stage is *hardening off*, when a plant becomes adjusted to the outdoor environment before it is set out. In sowing seeds you will take into consideration the growing conditions: soil mix, moisture, light and heat. These environmental factors will determine your success, but the process of seeding is not difficult or mysterious. Just think of seeding in the wild—plants propagate themselves fairly well. You, on the other hand, have to purchase seed and thereby hope to get as many plants as possible from each packet. Following a few rules will accomplish this and make seeding enjoyable.

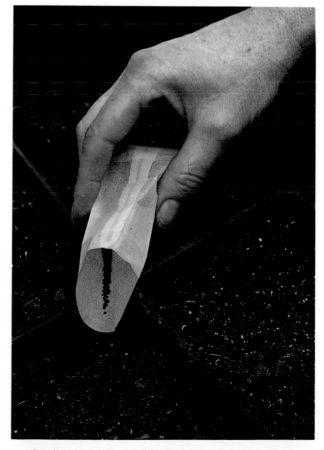

Seeding is the first step in the process of cultivation.

Seeding Containers

Any kind of seeding container can be used as long as it is at least two inches deep and has drainage holes for water to escape. We have used homemade wooden boxes, egg cartons, Styrofoam cups, manufactured plastic "flats" and plug trays. Also available on the market are compressed-peat-moss cubes that expand after watering. These often have some fertilizer added and may be used for seeding individual seeds without future transplanting.

Soils

Although one can purchase commercial soilless mixes, we prefer to mix our own. That mix is composed of one part sterilized garden soil (heat the soil in a covered pot at approximately 200° F for two hours to eradicate weed seeds and fungi), two parts peat moss and one part vermiculite (fine horticultural-grade crushed mica). For us, it has the best combination of ingredients for germinating seeds and maintaining seedlings for a period of time before we have to set them out into the field.

A seeding mixture should have the following characteristics: (1) It should be porous to allow excess water to percolate out and to allow the roots of germinating plants to grow freely. (2) It should have a sufficient amount of clay particles to hold the soil mix together and to retain moisture (soil should adhere to the roots when the plants are taken out of the containers). (3) It should contain enough nutrients, including trace minerals, to maintain a plant until it is transplanted to a larger container. Mixtures that have garden soil (advantageous because it contains trace minerals) tend to produce stronger plants and dry out less quickly if exposed to the sun for long periods of time. Mixtures that have a sufficient quantity of peat moss and vermiculite do not become compacted or offer resistance to the growing roots and root hairs.

Preparing a Flat for Seeding

To prepare a flat for seeding, you should fill it with a soil mix. Tamp it down to create a smooth level surface. This surface should be no lower than a half inch below the top of the container. A smooth surface creates a stable oxygenated micro-environment once the seedlings germinate.

Whether you place your seeds to germinate under lights, on a windowsill or in a greenhouse, you will try to use the space efficiently, growing as many plants within a given space as possible. The number of seeds in a given area is called "density." The more seeds per area, the more dense the seeding. The object of seeding is to create a desirable environment—an environment that will sustain germinated seeds (seedlings) up to the stage when they are transplanted into

Our seeding and transplanting mixture contains two parts peat moss, one part garden soil, and one part vermiculite.

The density of seeds in a flat has to be such that when the seeds germinate, the plants do not crowd each other.

larger containers. Therefore, the density of the seeds in a flat has to be such that, when the seeds germinate, the available space is well used but the plants do not crowd each other.

The rule of thumb to use in seeding is that with very fine seeds (such as those of mints, poppies or *Heuchera*) you should have no more than four seeds per square inch of surface. Larger seeds (such as those of *Helipterum roseum, Moluccella* or *Gomphrena*) should be seeded at half that density. With lower density, each plant has more light, water, air and nourishment. Also, use several containers for seeding rare plants. If something happens to one container (if you spill it, for example) you still have another as a backup.

Sowing

Most seeds will germinate well if they are sown on top or near the surface of the soil. Sow fine seeds on top of the soil by sprinkling them lightly over the surface of the tamped-down soil mix. Press them down into the surface of the soil (without covering) with a smooth flat object. We use the bottom of another flat. With large seeds, you can follow the same procedure but, in addition, you should cover with a thin (one-eighth of an inch) layer of sphagnum or peat moss or any light sterile medium. The object of tamping down or covering the seed is to surround the seed with moisture that will encourage the breaking of the seed coat.

Watering

With a misting nozzle on a hose, water lightly. Let the water percolate down and repeat the operation several times if necessary. Sprinkle in small amounts so that there is no standing water in the container. The fine spray and repeated moderate watering are less likely to disturb the seeds from their position. If you do not have a fine-spray nozzle, you can reach the same objective by placing your seeded container in a baking pan filled with water. This will allow the moisture to penetrate from the bottom.

The lip around the container has a function. It prevents water from rolling off the surface before it has a chance to penetrate to the roots. For the same reason, level your containers. The presence of water in every grain of soil will assure the development of a full, strong, expansive root system.

The Function of Moisture

Moisture in the soil functions in two ways: it provides humidity to break down the seed coat (allowing the seed to germinate) and it provides a vehicle for food to be transported to the germinating seed. A seed is usually composed of the pericarp (the outer coat) and the endosperm and embryo (the future plant). Before the seed can germinate, that outer coat has to crack under pressure from the embryo and endosperm. As

Germinating seeds are delicate, requiring a moist, warm environment with ample air circulation.

Nozzles used for watering. The small nozzle on the right emits a light mist for the youngest seedlings. The nozzle in the middle is used for watering larger plants.

the embryo is activated by heat, light and moisture, and, to some extent, the presence of oxygen, the coat allows the moisture to penetrate inside.

The seed starts germinating. This is the most delicate stage of growth because a seed, at this point, breaks its dormancy. It takes a chance that the environment will be favorable. Consequently, it is important to keep the germinated seedling from getting too dry. You should water germinating seeds when you notice that the surface or the bottom of the seed container seems to be drying out.

The Function of Air

Water is an important constituent of the soil mix. Air is also. When soil is watered too much, the particles of soil become congested much the same way lungs get congested. Little air or oxygen is able to penetrate to the seeds. Seeds in a waterlogged soil containing little or no oxygen may not germinate—a mechanism that allows some weed seeds to survive in the soil for as long as eighty years.

After germination, oxygen is necessary for respiration, for the development of roots and for the health of the plant. A small fan, blowing gently over the tops of germinated seedlings, often aerates the surface of the soil without stressing the plants. Air circulation is an important factor both in the greenhouse and in the field. The native habitat of many everlastings is an arid environment. There, the winds and the sun dehydrate any fungi that thrive in high humidity. Duplicating such conditions assures stronger plants. In the greenhouse the use of fans is essential. In the field this aeration is accomplished by the winds.

The Function of Heat

The seed coat of most everlastings will begin to crack in three days to two weeks. The warmer the temperature of the soil, the more quickly the seed coat will soften and crack. The warmer the temperature, the more quickly the

cotyledon will be able to break through the seed coat. Heat, in the moist environment of the seed, functions as a catalyst in softening the seed coat. During germination, temperature should not fluctuate widely. In most cases it should be between 65° F and 75° F. After the seed germinates, the growing temperature may be somewhat reduced.

For constant temperature during germination, try using a heat mat. Heat mats give even, thermostatically controlled heat. They are well worth the investment. It is bottom heat, rather than heat from the ambient air, that germinates seeds more efficiently, safely and quickly. Heat mats are used by many professionals.

The Function of Light

Although a few seeds prefer to germinate in the dark, most seeds require light to germinate. During development, light is crucial for photosynthesis and proper nutrient intake. Plants with sufficient exposure to light will have strong dark green stems and leaves. Light works in conjunction with nutrients (fertilizer) in the soil. The ratio of more light than nutrition will produce shorter plants. The ratio of more nutrition than light will produce tall, leggy plants.

Plants may be raised under fluorescent or tungsten lights. These lights, however, should have the light spectrum balanced for proper plant growth. Because neither fluorescent nor tungsten lights are as powerful as the sun, plants have to be exposed to artificial light for a longer period of time—preferably up to sixteen hours per day. The intensity is also important. Fluorescent fixtures should be within six inches of the plants to be effective. Since rays of the sun are intense, newly developing seedlings should be shielded from the noontime sun.

Fertilizing

During the earliest stages of growth the plant has a sufficient food supply stored in the cotyledon to keep it healthy. The cotyledon is a seed leaf. A true leaf, in most cases, differs from the seed leaf in shape and in structure; a seed leaf, for instance, may be more round and bulky than the true leaf. As the plant grows its first two sets of true leaves, it progressively exhausts its food supply. At this point, and throughout its growth, it needs more food.

You may want to consider fertilizing your seedlings with a very weak solution (perhaps one-twentieth of the standard dose) of a balanced soluble fertilizer. Fertilize every third or fourth time that you water because watering washes out fertilizer. It is much better to fertilize more often with a weak solution than to fertilize less often with a strong solution. Strong solutions may burn the leaves or roots of tender young plants.

As the plant grows larger, it will use nourishment and water more rapidly. The larger the plant, the more it transpires, the more it drinks. During hot and sunny days, water loss will be immense. The plant may need to be watered twice a day. Always water a drooping plant thoroughly, allowing the plant to regain sufficient turgidity to stand up. Fertilize only if the plant is already moist.

TRANSPLANTING

As seeds germinate, they become seedlings. First cotyledons come up and the roots go into the soil. Then the first set of true leaves shows up. Now is the time for the second stage in the seeding process—transplanting.

In transplanting we provide each seedling with enough room, light, air and nutrition to reach the size of approximately six inches in height during the next stage of growth. Now each plant has approximately four square inches of soil that is two inches deep. Eventually, the roots of the plants will penetrate to every corner of the flat, but this soil will sustain the plant, quite often, for more than two months.

Seedlings are transplanted from the seedling container to a new container—from a seed flat to the growth flat. Prepare your work space and the soil that is to receive the seedling much as you prepared the seeding flat. Pattern the planting of the seedlings in a new flat to accommodate the

After the plant develops the first set of true leaves, it is transplanted into a larger container where it has more room to grow.

plant. Make a hole all the way to the bottom of the flat with a dibble or your finger.

Separate the seedlings by carefully breaking up the soil in the original seeding flat. Slowly and gently separate out the plants so that each is now unattached to its previous neighbors. Hold the seedlings by leaves rather than stems whenever possible. If a leaf breaks, a new one will replace it. If a stem breaks, the plant will not regenerate.

Plants that have crowns growing out of a basal cluster (such as *Limonium* or *Heuchera*) should be planted at the same level at which the original seedling was planted. Plants which have tall stems with leaves up high (such as *Tagetes*, marigold) may be buried more deeply—up to the cotyledon. They will send out more roots on the stem. These roots will increase food-intake potential and will create a stronger, more vigorous plant. Gently tamp down the soil around the transplanted seedling in order to reduce the possibility of air pockets (air pockets dry out the roots). Now water in the same manner as you did newly sown seeds. During transplanting, keep the roots of seedlings moist.

Some Pointers for the Maintenance of Seedlings

Seedlings are fairly hardy plants that are likely to perform well. Rarely will there be any problems if you use common sense. The difficulty that many beginners encounter has to do with watering. We have found that if watering is done thoroughly, rather than superficially, there will be minimal problems. When water penetrates the top layer but does not percolate through holes in the bottom, plants develop weak, superficial roots.

During times of stress—heat shock, for example—plants with weak roots may perish from dehydration. Plants that are watered less often, but thoroughly, should develop roots that penetrate down. These roots serve the plant well. They protect it from shock and are instrumental in a quick recovery if the plant suffers a sudden water loss from either wind or heat. Watering should be done in the morning to allow moisture to evaporate from the leaves by the afternoon.

Complete watering produces deep root systems, which have the resilience to withstand such stress as drought or setting out into the field.

Watering in the afternoon encourages the growth of fungi at the cooler temperatures of the night.

By the same token, the surface of the soil should be relatively dry. When the seeds germinate, their stalks prevent air from circulating at the soil surface. Thus, air cannot help the plants at the level of the soil surface to stay dry. If the surface is too moist, germinating seedlings are susceptible to a condition called damping-off. Damping-off is a disease that is caused by a variety of fungi that prefer high-humidity and low-oxygen micro-environments. What actually happens is that the stems of emerging or growing plants become soggy at ground or below ground level. Stems rot. However, if the soil level is close to the edge of the container, the air has a greater chance to make its way around the plants and, consequently, oxygenate the soil and reduce ambient humidity.

HARDENING OFF

The seedling grows larger. As time passes, it begins to resemble the mature plant. Soon it may even start budding. Yet the plant is still in a protected environment. And outdoors is still too cool. This is the time when you should start thinking about getting your plants ready for the garden. You get the plant accustomed to the transition from the relative equilibrium of the indoors—constant temperature, humidity and moisture—to a relatively violent environment of the outdoors by "hardening it off."

Hardening off is accomplished in three successive steps that take place over a period of about four to five days. First, accustom the plant to temperature fluctuation. Allow the plant to be cool at night and warm during the day (however, do not expose the plant to temperatures below 40° F).

Second, after two days, start taking the plant outdoors, into a shady or sheltered spot, to allow the wind to whisk over its leaves. Wind pulls the moisture out of the leaves, lightly dehydrating the plant. Be sure, however, that the soil is thoroughly moist. The plant now gets used to the demands of its future environment. But bring it indoors if the temperature at night dips into the thirties.

The third and last stage of hardening off requires the plant to be under greater stress. Place the plant in full sun, with the wind blowing over the leaves and the outdoor temperature as low as 50° F. In stages, with selective application of stress, the plant will be ready for the field.

A few days before you set the plant out into the field you may allow the soil to dry out. Lightly drooping leaves are acceptable. Burned tips are not. Immediately before setting the plants out, water them to a point where the soil is dripping wet.

This process assures that when the plant is set out into the field, with the sun, the wind, the cold, the insects and the fungi ready to take their toll, it will be resilient, strong and ready. During hardening off, the leaves become fibrous, the stem gets woody, the roots grow sturdy. It is more difficult for insects and fungi to penetrate fibrous or woody tissue, and the wind and the sun are less likely to dehydrate a plant with an extensive root system that can rapidly replenish its moisture.

A PRODUCTION GARDEN

Preparation

Once the seedlings are hardened off, they are ready for the garden. But is the garden ready for the seedlings? During the last stages of spring, while the seedlings are growing and hardening off, the garden has to be prepared. You can think of a garden as a more expansive indoors. The environment is more difficult to control, but the elements are the same. The plant will need soil, heat, light and moisture. Everlastings are particular in their desire for light. Many come from sunny climates. Many perform especially well in rich moist soil. But even those whose native home is plains or a dry environment will produce more foliage and flowers on rich soil than in their native habitat.

Both annuals and perennials should have well-prepared soil if they are to produce well. Annuals need well-worked soil with a ready supply of nutrients and especially a high nitrogen

Hardening off is a process of adapting a plant to environmental stress.

Lime, compost and manure are tilled into the soil to nourish plants and to assure abundant crops later in the season.

content, because it is the nitrogen that encourages turgidity, foliage and flowers. For perennials the needs are similar. In order to grow and produce well, plants need well-prepared soil with lots of nutrition. The only difference between annuals and perennials in their soil requirements is that annuals must have a ready access to nitrogen during the whole summer. They may even need to be side-dressed or fed through the foliage. Perennials with excessive nitrogen may not be winter-hardy. Excessive nitrogen during the late months of summer counteracts the natural tendency of perennials to go dormant, increases their moisture content and makes them more susceptible to winter stress. Resist fertilizing or side-dressing perennials after the end of July.

Good soil nutrition is essential to plant health and vigor. Although nutrients such as nitrogen, potassium, phosphorus and trace elements are important, their availability to the plant is controlled to some extent by soil acidity. Soil acidity, in technical terms, is expressed by its pH number. The pH has a range from 0 to 14. Numbers above pH 7 designate an alkaline or basic soil. Numbers below pH 7 designate an acidic soil. Soil with pH 7 is neutral.

For most everlastings, soil pH should be between pH 6.5 and pH 7. Soil that is too acid, say below pH 6, will not have sufficient nutrients available to the plant to keep it healthy. Soil that has a high pH value may create an environment that is more hospitable to various soil-borne fungi. Soil pH may be adjusted according to your needs but it must be based upon an accurate measurement. With the help of either a do-it-yourself kit or a laboratory specializing in soil tests, you can add an appropriate combination of nutrients to your garden. The local Extension Service or the Department of Agriculture can guide you to what is available in your area.

A great variety of plants will not only survive

Plastic mulches warm the soil, control weeds and moderate soil temperature fluctuation.

but thrive in a rich soil environment. But so will plants that you do not particularly seek. We could dub them "weeds," for lack of a better word. They may actually be desirable (see Chapter 5). But for now, it will suffice to say that weeds in a garden are in constant competition for resources—the elements required for growth and maintenance of cultivated plants. In the garden, they are uninvited guests. It is costly in time and energy to maintain your cultivated plants and to reduce the competition from weeds, but the richer the soil, the more you will have to deal with weeds.

When we began gardening, we prepared our plot so that the soil had plenty of humus. The organic matter supplied by the addition of compost and manure encouraged finicky plants to produce great harvests and to ward off insects and disease. During the dry weather, humus holds moisture. During times of excess moisture, humus allows water to percolate into the

substrata. Humus is food for earthworms, which work the soil to break up compacted particles, allowing roots to penetrate and grow. It is also a source of trace minerals. Unfortunately, with good soil, even reluctant weeds found their way to the garden and soon we were unable to cope with maintenance. As soon as cultivated plants started to produce, we had no time left for weeding. Consequently, many crops were lost.

Mulches

We have always attempted to grow more plants than we were able to maintain. And we have always been in search of better ways to maintain a garden, including experimenting with mulches. Mulches reduce the population of weeds by stifling them out; reduce evaporation of moisture from the soil by creating an insulating barrier; and, simultaneously, reduce temperature fluctuation of the soil—resulting in a lower stress to the plant.

There are two kinds of mulches, hot and cold. Examples of hot mulches would primarily include brown, translucent and black plastics. (Recently, a black paper mulch has been developed and used successfully.) These mulches, in addition to performing the above functions, also warm the soil. Depending on the mulch, soil temperature may be warmed from ten to fifteen degrees above ambient temperature. The advantage of hot mulches is that they increase the metabolism of the plant and, thereby, its yield. The disadvantage of plastic mulches is that they are not biodegradable.

Examples of cold mulches are newspapers, hay, straw, seaweed and wood shavings. Cold mulches insulate the soil from the sun and moderate the warming of the soil. That quality is especially advantageous in hot, dry climates. Cold mulches are also useful because they are biodegradable. They contribute humus to the soil and they become food for earthworms. But in northern climates, cold mulches actually reduce production. Because they keep the soil at lower temperatures, plants metabolize at a slower rate. If you desire higher production, cold mulches are not for you.

Both kinds of mulches have advantages and disadvantages. Neither is a panacea. Let us look at plastic mulches first. The clear plastic mulch heats the soil the most. It works on the principle of the greenhouse effect. Heat that goes through the plastic is trapped. The soil underneath is the direct recipient of the sun's heat. However, a clear plastic mulch is not selective as to which plant life is spurred in growth. All plants germinate and grow rapidly, both weeds and cultivated plants. We have observed clear plastic straining from the pressure exerted by the vigorous growth of weeds. Clear plastic, for this reason, was designed to be used in conjunction with herbicides. For us, in our organic garden, the use of herbicides was neither desirable nor possible. Even if everlastings were tolerant to these compounds, and they are not, weeds would not compel us to resort to herbicides. Actually, many everlastings are weeds of one sort or another and would not tolerate any specific or broad-spectrum herbicides.

Brown plastic mulch, advertised as "photodegradable," will also absorb heat, although not to the same extent as clear plastic mulch. "Photodegradable" means that the plastic will break down into chunks upon exposure to sunlight. There are different sensitivities of photodegradable plastic—grades that break down at different rates, such as 90- or 120-day sensitivity. Farmers who do not enjoy pulling out used black plastic from the garden prefer brown plastic. Nevertheless, "photodegradable" does not mean "biodegradable." Brown plastic does not degrade but does break down, only on exposure to light and only into pieces that persist in their longevity. Those pieces that get mixed with the soil stay as chunks for ages. Other pieces of plastic fly about when the wind blows.

Black plastic mulch is not biodegradable. This factor should be regarded as valuably advantageous. Black plastic stays whole; it does not allow broad-leaf weeds to penetrate (an effective weed control without the use of herbicides); and it traps moisture. Although black plastic was designed to be utilized in conjunction with an irrigation system, you can achieve similar results if you lay the plastic after spring rains soak the ground. After a rain, black plastic traps moisture until it is later supplanted by periodic precipitation. Black plastic mulch is our choice. It can be used with both perennials and annuals. When used with perennials, it increases the survival of tender plants during harsh winters. We noticed that the survival rate of such tender plants as *Goniolimon* (German statice) and *Lavandula* (lavender) increased significantly. Production from these plants was also higher as compared with plants that were raised on soil without plastic mulch.

On the other hand, leaving black plastic mulch on the same patch of soil for many years does not allow for replenishment of either oxygen or organic matter. Depletion of oxygen in the soil causes an eventual decline in the health of your plants. The only solution to lack of nutrition and oxygen for a permanent bed of perennials is to move them every few years to newly refurbished ground. Although this is a tedious task, it is a trade-off between higher production with reduced necessity to weed and the extra work entailed in transplanting the plants to another spot. It should be noted that plastic chokes rapidly spreading perennials such as mints. If you do not consider this feature desirable, periodically enlarge the plastic holes through which the plants are growing.

When black plastic is used with annuals, neither oxygen depletion nor nutrient depletion is encountered. Over the span of one season, the soil stays friable and compaction is minimal. In the spring, when the plastic is removed and discarded, the whole process of manuring and liming is repeated. Mixing of nutrients and soil by harrowing or rototilling (with additional help from earthworms) keeps the soil airy and rich.

Laying Plastic Mulch

Our procedure for laying plastic mulch is as follows. In the spring, we first remove the plastic of the previous year. By keeping the plastic undisturbed over the winter, we reduce the possibility of soil erosion. Then we prepare the soil with manure and lime. Manuring in the spring puts all the available nourishment into the soil, and there is minimal loss due to leaching.

Subsequently, we harrow the vegetative remains and make raised beds by mounding the soil to a height of about eight inches and a width of about three feet. In creating raised beds, we accomplish three things. By scraping the highly nutritious topsoil into a mound, we deliver fertility to plants that need it most—plants that are cultivated. By mounding the soil, we create more surface area for the collection of heat from the sun. By placing plants higher into the air, we expose them to more air circulation—reducing the chance of mildew or the proliferation of fungi during the humid warm summer months.

After rains drench the soil, we lay the plastic. The plastic that we prefer to use is mulching grade—1.5 mil, four feet wide and textured (as opposed to one with a smooth shiny finish). The plastic is stretched tightly to prevent it from fluttering in the wind. Then the edges are

Paper and hay mulches cool the soil, reduce evaporation and provide a comfortable walking surface between plant rows.

anchored with soil or rocks (rocks are our most plentiful spring crop) every ten feet. Preferably, this is all done two weeks before planting time. During this period, the soil underneath the plastic is heated. This additional heat germinates weed seeds, but since the weeds have no light or air circulation, they all perish. When we get ready to plant, the potential weed population has been substantially reduced.

Between the raised rows covered with black plastic we now have shallow valleys. This area will be used for walking. But it cannot be left alone, for weeds will germinate rapidly and creep into the space of the raised bed. To avoid this problem, we mulch between rows as well. However, here we place sheets of newspapers (avoiding colored and clay-coated paper because heavy metals may have been used in the inks) and, on top of the newspapers, a layer of hay.

Newspapers should overlap each other and the sloping sides of the plastic-covered raised beds so that germinating weed seeds are denied access to light. Since the newspapers are dry and are apt to be dislodged by the wind, the hay layer functions as an anchor until such time as rains and moisture conform the newspapers to the shape of the soil.

Newspapers create a barrier to germinating weeds that is far more effective than hay or straw alone. At the same time, newspapers and hay allow moisture to percolate down. Combining the two also prevents a high rate of water evaporation from the soil. As a bonus, the space between the rows of plants becomes a pleasant surface on which to walk. Growing plants stand out against the hay, giving an appearance of a tapestry. By the end of the season the newspapers will have disintegrated, and by spring the newspaper-and-hay composite will have become humus—food for plants and worms in subsequent years.

There is one objection that has been raised to using hay, as opposed to straw, in the garden. People often ask, "Doesn't hay contribute to the weed problem? Would it not be better to use straw and not add excessive weeds to the garden?" Hay does contain weed seeds, but every time the wind blows over the garden, it deposits a goodly amount of weed seeds anyway. Weed seeds are omnipresent. Even in the soil they may survive for as long as fifty years without germinating. Thus, how would you quantify the concept of "excessive" weeds? The problem of using hay and contributing "excessive" weeds to the garden seems to be primarily a problem of semantics.

Setting Out in the Field

Setting plants or seedlings out into the field requires the same care as transplanting in the greenhouse. As we set out each plant, we poke a hole through the plastic. Holes should be large enough to accommodate the plant and spacious enough to prevent damage to leaves from plastic heated by the sun. Conversely, they should be small enough to limit the number of weeds which may come up around the plant.

We bury the seedlings according to the same procedure that we discussed in the section on transplanting. Plants that have crowns are buried to the same level as they were in the flat. Plants that have long stems may be buried up to the first set of leaves. These stems will set out roots, anchoring the plant and allowing a greater intake of nutrients.

Each kind of plant is set out in a pattern according to the amount of space it will take up when it becomes mature in late July. The row is

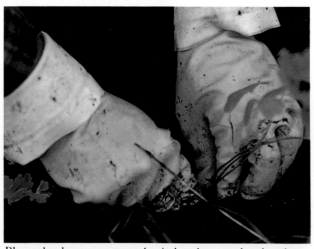

Plants that have crowns are buried to the same level as they were in the original container.

The best times for setting out plants in the field are cloudy and rainy days, when there is the least chance for plants to be set back due to stress.

three feet wide, but the pattern varies depending on the type of plant. It may be one and then two or two and then three. Rarely, and only if the plants are large—e.g., *Artemisia annua*, which grows to five feet in height and three feet in diameter—do we plant it in an offset one-one pattern. At first, plants on plastic look small and insignificant. By the end of July, however, there is just enough room to walk between rows. The rows are like hedges. Plants extend and blend into each other, hiding any evidence of plastic. And the garden, a green carpet, is woven with intricate accents of color.

Rotating Crops

In garden areas where we plant annuals, we do not reuse plastic mulches. There are two reasons for this. First, each plant has a different pattern for planting. Since we vary the number of plants from year to year, we could not match the same spaces. Second, and a more important reason, is that we rotate our crops. Every year the location of a particular plant is changed. Consequently, when the plastic is taken off, it is invariably damaged and cannot be reused.

Crop rotation is not a new concept. Based on diligent record keeping of plant locations in previous years, it is an indispensable technique in striving for healthy soil and plants. There is substantial evidence that plant diseases persist in soils that are repeatedly cropped with the same family of plants. Plants of the same family usually require similar nutrients. They also are prone to similar diseases. For instance, plants of the cabbage family, Cruciferae, are apt to get clubroot, caused by *Plasmodiophora brassicae*, a fungus that destroys roots. The only way to control this disease is to burn infected plants and/or to rotate crops. But once clubroot becomes established, Cruciferae plants should not be placed in that spot for a period of up to five years.

The pattern of plant-specific nutrient use is common to related plants (yet another reason to learn botanical names). If specimens of the same family are planted in the same area year after

During a rainy period, plants that were set through holes poked in the plastic mulch create an instant garden.

Each species is set out in a pattern according to the amount of space it will take up when it becomes mature in late July.

By the end of July, there is just enough room to walk between rows.

year, certain nutrients are bound to be depleted. The potential for disease will increase. When disease is present, it is difficult to eradicate. The old adage "An ounce of prevention is worth a pound of cure" applies to keeping a garden healthy and productive.

Maintenance

If you have ever had a garden, you know perfectly well that work does not stop with the planting of seedlings. The garden must be maintained. A significant part of maintenance is weeding. In an unmulched garden, weeds sprout everywhere. In a mulched garden, weeds sprout up in places where the soil is exposed to light.

Weeds may be wild plants that compete with cultivated crops. Or they may be rapidly spreading perennials. In either case, there is competition for light, moisture, air and nutrients. Weeds, by their nature, can outcompete cultivated plants. Their competition must be checked if you are to get any production.

Weeding is a delicate and intricate undertaking. If not done carefully, it can cause more harm than good. When weeds are two to four inches tall, they are easy to see and easy to pull out. But when they branch out and get much larger than six to eight inches, they have already established an extensive root system that reaches well beyond the stem of the weed.

If a weed is contiguous to a cultivated plant, pulling on the weed may disturb the roots of your cultivar. Cultivars are delicate plants. Any disturbance will surely cause injury—dieback, weakness, susceptibility to insects or, certainly, a gradual but total decline of the plant. At the stage when weeds are large, they should be cut off with shears at ground level or below the first set of leaves. By the time the weed sports another head, the summer may nearly be over. Weeding is easiest when the soil is moist. The roots seem to slip out when you pull. When the ground is dry, weeds are entrenched and are held back by the compacted desiccated soil granules. Pulled weeds are a suitable compost material.

Although weeds are hardly desirable, they can play a positive role in a garden. For example, they distract insects from cultivated crops. Wild mustards distract cabbage butterflies from cabbages; lamb's-quarters (*Chenopodium album*) takes its share of flying aphids. You can also think of weeds as green manure. When plowed in, they decompose and refurbish the soil. Weeds with deep taproots enrich the topsoil by bringing nutrients up from below. When these weeds die, they leave spaces through which water percolates. For us, perhaps the best contribution of weeds is that many are superb everlastings; *Solidago* (goldenrod), for example, is a basic filler for many arrangements. As Ella Wheeler Wilcox suggested: "A weed is but an unloved flower!"

Another aspect of garden maintenance is the control of insect damage. The word "control" is used advisedly. Insects cannot and should not be eradicated. Even deleterious insects are part of the delicate balance of nature. They are food for birds and other, beneficial insects. They consume plants that are weak due to stress—drought, poor nutrition or genetic constitution. Actually, this may be a desirable feature. Weak plants are cleaned out to allow the hardier, more resistant plants to propagate the species.

Plants that have good nutrition are more resistant to insect damage. That is why soil preparation and nutrient replenishment is so critical. Crop rotation is also a good practice in controlling damage from insects. An adjunct to crop rotation is polyculture, a scheme of planting many diverse species of plants in one area. Monoculture, on the other hand, is exemplified by large tracts of land under a single crop. A dense population of a plant or animal species encourages disease and devastating epidemics. Polyculture creates difficulties for insects. Insects become confused with distractions. Moreover, with polyculture, there are fewer individuals of any one species of plant to host an invasion. And when plants are mixed, it is more difficult for insects to locate their target.

But, let's face it, there may be a preponderance of insects that may ruin your plants. If you must use insecticides, you should be conservative. There are several reasons for our opposition to the indiscriminate use of pesticides. Insecticides may be harmful not only to target insects but also to beneficial insects. Moreover, heavy insecticide use on immense populations of insects allows those that have genetic immunity to propagate and to pass on to their progeny the immune characteristics. The history of the use of pesticides and antibiotics is replete with stories of such developments. What man creates, nature subverts. New chemicals must constantly be developed to counteract nature's tendencies to protect its own.

For these reasons, we do not periodically spray our garden "just in case." We do not panic when we see a flea beetle on our *Gomphrena*. We do, however, carefully examine the plants daily. We collect egg masses from the surface or from under the leaves. And when we use insecticides, we try to catch insects in their larval stages. When they are small, they are more susceptible. When they are adults, they are more resistant.

The sprays that we use are biodegradable and are effective only for a short time. We have used three kinds of sprays: (1) rotenone and pyrethrum combinations on beetles and aphids, (2) *Bacillus thuringiensis* (a bacterium) on larvae of moths and butterflies and (3) insecticidal soap solutions on aphids and wax-coated insects. Pyrethrum is manufactured from *Chrysanthemum cinerarifolium* (a daisy), and rotenone is derived from a plant of the genus *Derris*. Both are contact poisons that are useful on soft-bodied insects. However, they are also poisonous to bees and to cold-blooded animals such as fish and frogs and snakes. Apply this insecticide only on the target insect and watch out for bees. The second insecticide is a bacterium that behaves like a stomach poison. It is specific to larvae of moths and butterflies and is not harmful to beneficial insects or to cold-blooded animals. The third insecticide, soap, coats insects and prevents them from breathing.

Spraying should be done just as insects hatch. Insecticides should also be applied early in the morning, before bees and other pollinators work the flowers. Conservative use of insecticides, even if they are biodegradable, in the long run will create fewer problems for the environment and you.

Praying mantis eats aphids and other insects injurious to cultivated plants.

Another way to deal with harmful insects is to introduce them to their enemies—praying mantises, ladybugs, trichogramma wasps, green lacewings or predatory midges. These beneficial insects are biologically safe agents for controlling garden pests. But don't be surprised when they move on to better hunting grounds once their food supply becomes scarce.

HARVESTING

Harvesting is our favorite task because it is a process of complex and intricate decision making that is based on intimate knowledge of a plant. Harvesting takes into consideration environmental conditions—the humidity of the air and the amount of moisture in the soil—as well as the developmental characteristics of the flowering plant. What makes picking pleasant is that with each flower one has to make a decision as to the maturity and potential development of the flower after picking. There is no simple answer to the question "When do I pick everlastings?" Each flower or pod should be picked at its own particular time. Some flowers are picked when they are mature; others, before maturity.

Nevertheless, over the past decade, we have derived some general rules for the picking of all everlastings. These rules are based on observations of all kinds of flowers—daisy-shaped,

Statice is picked as soon as most of the spike is developed. Flowers on tips open a bit as the flower dries.

spiked, inherently moist and seemingly dry. There are five categories of flowers, from the wild or a cultivated garden, suitable as everlastings. When you pick, you will have to fine-tune each rule according to the ecology of the plant—whether it grows in moist soil, whether you are harvesting after rain or whether there is a dry spell. On the other hand, once you know a rule, you will be able to extrapolate picking information from one flower to another flower within that category.

Rules for Picking

The first category applies to daisy-like and spiked flowers that open after picking. A good example in this category is the well-known straw-flower (*Helichrysum*). When the bud is picked as the first set of petals opens up, the flower will open in drying to a stage where the center is still tight but the petals show their iridescent color.

To the second category belong flowers that contract after picking. A good example here is *Ageratum*. When the open heads contract, the color intensifies. *Ageratum* should be picked when the center bud is almost totally developed and the side buds are just beginning to open up. If the flower is picked too early, it will contract and an insufficient amount of color will show. If picked when the flower is ready to go to seed, it will dry but will shatter in handling. All the seeds will puff out and there will be nothing but calyx left.

An example of the third category of everlastings is *Xeranthemum*—which some call immortelle, a flower after which the immortelles were named. This flower stays exactly the same as when you pick it. If picked in bud, it will remain in bud. If picked fully open, it stays fully open. Moisture and humidity do not seem to affect it. On the other hand, the petals are fragile and will bend at the slightest pressure. *Xeranthemum* should be hung right after picking. If it is placed to rest on its petals, even that negligible weight will crease the petals, rendering the dried flower quite useless.

The fourth category is exemplified by a flower which has a "life of its own." Acroclinium (*Helipterum roseum*), when on the plant, opens and closes. Its behavior depends on light and humidity. When the day is dark, cloudy or very humid, the flower closes up. When the day is dry or sunny, the flower opens up. Features of this pattern remain for years after the flower has been picked and dried. Even indoors, when the air is humid, the flower closes up into a loose bud. When the air is dry, as in the winter, the flower folds its petals back toward the stem. *Helipterum roseum* should be picked either in the late bud stage—as it will open somewhat in drying—or in the very early flowering stage. If picked later than two days after it initially shows its center, it may shatter in handling.

The last category concerns spikes or racemose flowers, which are borne on a central stem and which open sequentially either toward the top or toward the bottom of the stem. The more common spike-type flowers open from the bottom: *Delphinium*, *Salvia* and *Lavandula* are perfect examples. Others, fewer in number, open from the top: *Liatris* (blazing-star) and *Spiraea tomentosa* (steeplebush).

The object in picking spikes is to get as many side flowers and as much color as possible. Spikes that open from the bottom up should be picked when approximately two-thirds to four-fifths of the spike is developed but before the bottom flowers begin to fade. Spikes that open from top down should be picked just before the flowers at the top start going by. If picked later, the tips shatter and become unattractive. Fur-

Blue salvia is a valuable source of true blue color for
wreaths and arrangements.

Conditions for Drying

Once flowers are harvested, they should be
dried and stored for future use. The time it takes
to dry a flower depends on when it is picked
(after a rain or during a dry spell); on how much
moisture there is in the flower (*Helichrysum* will
dry more slowly than *Limonium latifolium*, sea
lavender); and on the relative humidity of the
drying environment (whether it is a hot attic or a
cool garage). Drying, depending on these factors,
may take anywhere from a few days to two
weeks. But, generally speaking, it is not advantageous to have flowers drying for a long period
of time. The longer the drying time, the more
deterioration one observes.

The rule of thumb that you should apply to
drying any everlasting flower is that the more
quickly you dry the flower, the better you will
preserve the color and shape. To get the best
color and shape, you should hang the flowers in
an environment with low humidity, high ambient
temperature, adequate air circulation and limited
incident light (reflected light does not affect
color to the same degree as direct light; direct
light with a high ultraviolet component will
bleach flowers). Each of these factors influences
the quality of the everlasting.

In environments with high humidity, such
as cellars or sheds with soil floors, flowers may
mold rather than dry. Color deteriorates to a
point where it is dull or musty brown. The trick
is to have atmospheric humidity lower than that
in the vicinity of the drying flower, so that
moisture dissipates from the flower into the air.

One way to achieve this is to have dehumid-
ifiers in the drying area. By far, a better and less
costly way to accomplish the same goal is to have
the flowers in small bunches hanging where
temperature is higher than that of the outdoors.
A hot, poorly insulated attic is ideal. During the
day, it may get to 115° F. A temperature between
100° F and 130° F is desirable. Another option is
to dry flowers in a shed with a wood stove. By the
end of summer, when the days are cooler and
more humid, this kind of arrangement may prove
to be necessary.

Even when bunches are small and the air is

thermore, the top cannot be clipped off without
leaving the flower with a stubbly appearance.

The length of the stem on harvested flowers
depends on three considerations: how you plan
to use them; the distance between the flower and
other buds that will become flowers; and the
moisture content of the plant.

If you plan to use a particular flower only for
decorating a wreath, you may be satisfied with a
short stem. If you plan to use the flower for a tall
arrangement, you will need a longer stem. Since
it is to your advantage to collect as many flowers
as possible from any given plant and since most
plants develop further buds on the stems, you
should decide how many future buds you are
willing to sacrifice for a longer stem. Flowers that
have long stems and many leaves dry more
slowly than flowers on short stems with few
leaves.

warm, it is smart to use a small fan to keep air circulating. In a bunch, flowers on the outside are exposed to air but flowers on the inside are in a humid micro-environment. A fan aids in removing humidity from the central portion of a bunch. It would not at all be unusual to have a bunch of *Salvia farinacea* show beautiful blue on the outside but hide mold on the inside. The same conditions are pertinent to *Tagetes* (marigolds), *Celosia*, *Eupatorium* (Joe-Pye weed) and other flowers that are not true immortelles.

The last factor in drying everlastings concerns light. Many references indicate that you need to have a dark room to dry flowers successfully. We find this to be unnecessary. While it is true that sunlight rapidly bleaches certain kinds of flowers—e.g., *Gomphrena* and *Lavandula*—it does nothing to *Helichrysum* or *Consolida* (larkspur.) Sometimes it may even be desirable to put *Consolida* in sunlight to dry it more quickly. Once in a while we bring it into an empty greenhouse on a midsummer morning. By afternoon it may be dry. You should take it into a darker environment soon after it dries, but direct sunlight should not affect the color of *Consolida* in only two days of exposure.

A word of advice about light. The color of flowers is like the natural dye in upholstery. If you leave the flowers in direct hot sun, they will rapidly bleach out. If your light source is a tungsten light (as opposed to fluorescent light with a high ultraviolet component), deterioration will be minimal and slow. The same applies to the fragrance of herbs. Sunlight breaks down essential oils of decorative herbs. In direct light, *Lavandula* or *Artemisia* will acquire a neutral, innocuous straw-like fragrance instead of a pleasant pungency.

Tying and Hanging

When storing flowers you should look for a method that uses space efficiently, allows for convenient retrieval and minimizes losses due to breakage. We have tried and prefer a method in which flowers are bunched and hung from nails on a beam. When flowers are picked, they lose moisture and rigidity. If you have ever seen

Scabiosa stellata pods may be stored in a box because they are dry, sturdy and non-hygroscopic.

Small bunches of blue salvia are fastened with a rubber band and tied with a piece of twine. A poker makes it easy to hang the bunch on a nail.

wilting flowers in a vase, you can deduce what would happen if we dried flowers by standing them in a container. They would wilt and would dry with their heads drooping. If the flowers are hung to dry, they dry with stems and heads straight.

Some people store flowers in boxes. It is a satisfactory method for storing certain flowers only if they are already dry. But we have concluded that storing flowers in boxes is a risky proposition, especially if the flowers are highly hygroscopic (that is, readily absorb moisture from the air) and if the environment is likely to become humid. If you store *Salvia* in a box, for example, it may reabsorb moisture and mold. Or, with an outcome just as unfavorable, the weight of the stem and the flower may bend or squash petals.

Generally, flowers are bunched to save space and time in picking, storing and retrieving. Bunches are made by placing the stems of flowers neatly together, with the bottoms at the same level. Then the stems are tied with string, twine, rubber bands and the like. Bunches should be small enough to allow for consistent loss of moisture (preventing any possibility of rotting or molding) and large enough to take as little time as possible in tying. With *Salvia*, which is inherently moist, you would want a bunch of stems to be no more than half an inch in diameter. *Limonium* stems may be bunched to two inches in diameter.

As flowers dry, the stems lose moisture and shrink. If the bunches were tied only with a piece of string, the string would not adjust to the shrinkage. Consequently, flowers from such bunches will start falling onto the floor. On impact, flower heads will break. Bunches that are bound with a tight rubber band are more likely to accommodate shrinkage. This method of tying is best.

To tie a bunch, collect approximately half of the flowers of the finished bunch. Then drape a piece of a string (twelve inches long) one inch from the bottom of the stems. Collect the rest of the bunch and place it on top of the string, fit a rubber band around the bottom of the bunch and, finally, tie the ends of the string together. The string fits over a nail in a beam. When you

Flowers may be bunched not only for efficiency in storing and retrieving, but also for decoration.

need to retrieve a particular bunch, you can reach with a tip of a poker into the string and take the bunch off the nail. This process is quick and efficient. Once flowers are dry, you may place more flowers on top of a previous bunch. Because you use a poker to retrieve the bunches, you need not be seven feet tall or use a ladder.

When you start to grow and harvest everlastings you will discover that there is more and more to learn and do. The information given here is a reference point. It is inevitable that your particular gardening needs, your techniques and your preferences will be uniquely your own.

3
Annuals

Though annual flowers have to be replanted every year, the effort is well worth it, for the most intense colors, tones and shades in everlasting flowers come from annual plants. Moreover, everlastings with the most spectacular coloration and tonal variation come primarily from cultivated annual plants. For example, the whites of *Ammobium* and *Xeranthemum* are clear, almost iridescent whites. The blues of *Salvia farinacea* and *Centaurea cyanus* are true blues, unlike the grayish blue of *Lavandula* or the subdued hues of *Echinops ritro*. The reds of *Celosia* and *Salvia splendens* are striking reds, colors unlike anything found among perennials or shrubs.

Germany made it very fashionable during the nineteenth century, when it became a state flower.

The species *C. moschata* was introduced from Persia by way of Constantinople during the reign of Charles I of England. The flower of this species is finer, more delicate in form.

CULTIVATION: *Centaurea* grows rapidly. Therefore, it should not be seeded in the greenhouse until the middle of April, to be set out at the end of May. It transplants well and is hardy until the first heavy frost. As long as the abundant flowers are picked steadily, the plant will keep on producing. However, if unpicked, the plant will stop producing flowers and its energies will go into seed production. Some books suggest that one needs to have several successive sowings in order to maintain flower production. We find that unnecessary as long as the flowers are diligently picked and not allowed to go to seed.

PICKING: In order to get *Centaurea* to hold its color and shape, the flower must be picked within a half day of opening from the bud stage and then it must be dried as rapidly as possible. This is, perhaps, one of the most troublesome flowers to dry because the time of picking is so critical. If it is picked too late, the color of the bloom fades and the petals fall apart.

We have tried several methods of drying: hanging the flowers and allowing them to dry over a period of a few days; drying them on long stems and short; drying them in the oven the way one would dry parsley—at 150° F for approximately fifteen minutes. Dried in the oven, the flowers remain sturdy and the color is fast. This, of course, is much too tedious a method for drying a large quantity. We pick the largest

amount of our crop in the morning, and then the flowers are hung to dry at the very top of the attic, where the temperature reaches close to 130° F. Any flowers that shatter are sent to the potpourri basket, for they still retain good color.

Chenopodium botrys
AMBROSIA

COMMON NAMES: ambrosia, oak of Jerusalem, feather-geranium.
HISTORY: Most of the 250 species of *Chenopodium* are weedy. The plant is native to Europe, Africa, and Asia but is now naturalized in North America. It is a close relative of the common garden weed *C. album* (lamb's-quarters or pigweed). The genus name is derived from the shape of the leaf, which resembles a goose foot. The species name implies that the flowers are in the form of grapes. According to Gerard, ancients supposed that this very fragrant herb was food for the gods. Medicinally, plants boiled in wine were used to relieve shortwindedness (perhaps the wine also had something to do with the cure). In the kitchen, leaves were used in conserves, in soups and in flavoring meats. The plant was also used as a moth repellent. Many legends surround the plant

in both Western and Eastern civilizations.

Another close relative, *C. ambrosioides* (Mexican tea), also has a pleasant aroma and is cultivated for its oil, which has medicinal properties.
CULTIVATION: In its production of seed, *Chenopodium* is similar to *Celosia*. As the plant dries, the seeds drop out, and they do so over a long period of time. Little special care is needed in growing the plant, which is tolerant to dry and hot weather. Seeding, however, requires special care because the seeds are so tiny that any disturbance to the soil will disrupt the germination process. Self-seeding (volunteering) is common, suggesting that the best way to propagate the plant is to seed lightly on the surface of the soil in the greenhouse seedling tray, or to let nature take its course in the garden.
PICKING: The whole plant should be cut down and hung up to dry before frost. If you want to collect seed, hang up a few plants inside a paper bag. As the plant dries, seeds will be shed into the bag. Like *Artemisia annua* or *A. schmidtiana*, *Chenopodium* may be brittle if used dry in a wreath. It is also possible to use it green by weaving a wreath and then placing the wreath on a shelf to dry. Allow plenty of room for air circulation to prevent molding.

Chrysanthemum ptarmiciflorum
DUSTY MILLER

COMMON NAMES: dusty miller, silver lace.
HISTORY: This plant used to be classified as *Pyrethrum* and is one of the many plants that bear the common name dusty miller. The botanical name *Pyrethrum* is an

allusion to the fiery taste of the roots of *Anacyclus pyrethrum*, a plant native to the Mediterranean region. *C. ptarmiciflorum* is native to the Grand Canary Island. In many warmer parts of the temperate regions, this white-flowering plant is a perennial and grows up to three feet. In cooler climates it is shorter and is used primarily as a foliage plant.

CULTIVATION: Seeds are easy to germinate, but are very small and should be planted sparsely enough not to crowd each other when they germinate. The woolly leaves of this plant are also subject to fungus and rot if they are kept overly moist.

PICKING: Picking of the foliage should take place well before frost because by that time the cool and moist days of fall will surely spoil the clean gray color. Once dry, the foliage is quite brittle, so it must be handled gently.

Consolida ambigua
LARKSPUR

COMMON NAMES: larkspur, annual delphinium, lark's toe, knight's spur.

HISTORY: *Consolida ambigua* is one of 40 annual species native to the Mediterranean and naturalized in Asia. It was classified under *Delphinium*, which contains some 300 species. The first to be introduced to England was *D. staphisagria* (Stavesaker) in 1551 and then *D. consolida*, described by Tusser in 1572 (valued as a wound herb). It is this species that is the parent to *C. ambigua*, a plant that is found wild in European cornfields. In a wide range of colors, including white, pink, lilac, rose and purple, this spike is often double-flowering. The common name comes from the shape of the

flower, which resembles a lark's spur or claw. According to some sources, the former genus name is from the Greek, meaning dolphin-like. *Ajacis* stands for Ajax; according to a classical legend, the plant was born from the blood of the slain Greek hero.

Although a tincture of the plant was used as a topical insecticide and the crushed petal juice with a bit of alum was used as ink, every part of the plant, including the seed, is very poisonous. Children should be watched carefully because ingestion of small amounts could cause vomiting. Ingestion of large amounts could result in death.

CULTIVATION: Like the perennial delphinium, larkspur should be seeded directly into the ground or into individual pots for setting out into the garden. If the plant is seeded in flats during transplanting, it is shocked beyond its ability to recover. Its roots are very sensitive.

PICKING: Pick when approximately four-fifths of the spike is open. With both annual and perennial delphiniums, we suspend the plants on individual clothespins on a wire and hang them in the greenhouse to dry. As soon as we sense that the petals are close to being dried, we tie a few in a bunch and hang them with all the other flowers. Larkspurs have a tendency to fall apart if they are not dried rapidly, and if they are bunched too closely together, the blooms become misshapen.

Cotula barbata
PINCUSHION PLANT

COMMON NAME: pincushion plant.

HISTORY: Cotula comprises 60 species, some annual, some perennial, which are members of the Anthemis tribe. Most are native to the Southern Hemisphere. A fairly inconspicuous little plant, *Cotula* was classified at first with *Anthemis*. Native to Africa, this flower resembles that of *Santolina* and smaller versions of petal-less species of *Chrysanthemum parthe-*

Gomphrena globosa

Alyssum, Salvia, Verbena

nium, feverfew. The etymology of the plant is uncertain. The genus name is derived from the Latin, but no reference can be found about its meaning. *Barbata* means bearded or barbed.

CULTIVATION: This is a fairly sensitive plant in that the roots are delicate and transplanting is not always successful. The seed will germinate readily, but the plant is sensitive to heat and dry soil. Be sure to keep it moist.

PICKING: The little button-like flowers can easily be dried by hanging. However, the plant is of dubious value for growing as a dry flower because it is so labor-intensive and its production, comparatively, is minimal. Pick when it is fully open or when two-thirds of the center has opened up.

Emilia javanica
TASSEL FLOWER

COMMON NAMES: tassel flower, Flora's paintbrush.

HISTORY: Most of the 20 species come from the Old World, some from the American tropics. Essentially, only one species is cultivated in home gardens. The flower resembles hawkweed (Indian paintbrush), but *Emilia* dries better and holds its shape.

CULTIVATION: The seeds germinate readily and the seedlings are

very sturdy. They do not experience any transplant shock, and as soon as they are established they bloom profusely. The plant must be harvested constantly if you want it to go on flowering.

PICKING: *Emilia* is difficult to pick primarily because there are several flowers on each head and each flower is at a different stage of development. Consequently, one has to pick for the happy medium—when the first flower has not gone by and the last flower is yet to open. Since this is a composite, the flower develops from the outside and goes by as soon as flowers in the middle have opened up. If it is picked at this stage, the center will puff out and there will be no color showing. If picked too early, the flower head closes up and reveals little color.

Eucalyptus cinerea
EUCALYPTUS

COMMON NAMES: eucalyptus, silver-dollar tree.

HISTORY: This tree is native to New South Wales and Victoria, Australia, and is hardy in zone 9, but will not survive soil temperatures below 25° F.

CULTIVATION: Easily started from seed at 70° F, this plant grows slowly at first but by the end of the summer it will send out several two- to three-foot side branches. Warmth, good soil and moisture are essential to good performance. In the fall, shortly before or after a light frost, dig up the whole plant and bring it into the house where it can be wintered over.

PICKING: Pick branches before the frost, leaving several leaf nodes for the plant to sprout new branches. There are three methods of drying eucalyptus: in a drying agent such as gel or sand; by hanging; by placing the stems in a mixture of two parts water and one part glycerine for approximately ten days. Eucalyptus preserved in glycerine is the best form for designing since the leaves remain soft and pliable.

Gomphrena globosa
and *G. haageana*
GLOBE AMARANTH

COMMON NAME: globe amaranth.

HISTORY: There exist over 100 species native to the Americas, Australia and Asia. Two varieties of *G. globosa* are usually described in seed catalogues: the standard variety, which we raise because of the long stems, and the dwarf variety, Buddy, which stands twelve inches tall. The orange species has an altogether different form; it is a smaller plant with many fewer blooms than *G. globosa*. The orange plant is also much more leggy than the white, pink and purple. A red variety has a conformation similar to the orange plant. The genus name is

derived from the Greek *gomphos*, a nail, wedge or club, in reference to the shape of the flower. *G. globosa* is a native of India.

CULTIVATION: Both species can easily be started from seed, but because the seeds are so large and, inside the bract, hairy, the seedlings have a tendency to damp off. They fare best when started at 80° F on a heat mat. A good cure for damping-off—a disease caused by a fungus in which the stem rots at the soil level—is to have plenty of air circulation. Either install a fan or place the flats in the sun (without letting the seedlings dry out) to reduce moisture at the surface of the soil.

After the seedlings are set out into the field, for the longest time they just sit getting acclimatized. Once the weather warms, the plants thrive and grow rapidly. Although the plants are as resilient as their cousins, the wild amaranths, they should not be planted where there is little air circulation, because in the heat

and humidity of August it is possible that they may develop mildew and fungus on the least exposed surfaces of the plants.

PICKING: These are frost-hardy plants. Toward the end of the growing season they withstand early light frosts (*G. haageana* is actually classified as a perennial). Usually they should be picked before the first frost, but with the inevitable rush to harvest all the delicate plants—*Celosia*, for example—we tend to procrastinate. It is only with a heavy frost that *Gomphrena* suffers injury. If the plant is allowed to set bracts throughout the summer, the flowers get larger and larger, with some reaching a length of two inches. Cut down the whole plant and use the blossoms as needed. Of all the colors, the orange is most susceptible to bleaching from reflected light.

Helichrysum bracteatum
STRAWFLOWER

COMMON NAMES: strawflower, everlasting, immortelle.

HISTORY: Perhaps as many as 500 *Helichrysum* species of annuals, perennials and shrubs are found in the Old World, Australia and South Africa. *H. bracteatum* is a native of Australia, from where it was introduced to England in 1799. Among the other species that produce flowers worth drying are: *H. belloides*, with half-inch white single flowers; *H. angustifolium*, with half-inch clusters of flowers of up to two inches (resembling *Gnaphalium obtusifolium*); *H. milfordiae*, with white glossy bracts one inch across; *H. plicatum* (like *H. angustifolium*); and *H. thianschanicum* (also like *H. angustifolium*).

The genus name comes from

heli, sun, and *chrysos*, golden. This is perhaps the best known of all the everlastings. Its common name, strawflower, has become synonymous with the genre. In fact, many catalogues list everlastings under "S," for strawflowers.

Certainly there are many helichrysums which resemble *Gnaphalium* and *Anaphalis* more than they resemble *H. bracteatum*. Most of those helichrysums have a hairy, cudweed appearance with small clusters of flowers on the top of the stem. *H. orientale* (golden mothwort), *H. stoechas* (golden Cassidony), *H. arenarium* (dwarf

Helichrysum bracteatum

yellow immortelle), *H. angustifolium*, *H. plicatum* and *H. petiolatum* very much resemble *Gnaphalium* except that the flowers of these are yellow or creamy white. Some species, *H. thianschanicum*, for instance, are quite fragrant with an odor of curry.

CULTIVATION: *H. bracteatum* is perhaps the largest of the species, often growing to a height of five feet. In fertile soil it produces abundant blooms beyond the first light frosts. During the heavy production of the summer months, it is a good idea to give the plant some foliar fertilizer with seaweed, fish emulsion or weak manure tea. This feeding assures a consistent quality bloom. Woolly-leaved helichrysums prefer dry and airy conditions in which to grow because they are quite susceptible to rot.

PICKING: *H. bracteatum* (and many other members of this genus) develops even after it is picked in the bud stage. The object is to pick the bud when it has reached the largest possible size without having de-

Helichrysum thianschanicum

veloped so far that, once dried, it will open to reveal its center. One should follow this guide: When the bud is still covered by leaves, it should not be picked. When the first row of petals begins to open up, it should be picked immediately. However, if the third row opens up, it may be too late to get a good dried blossom. Factors that determine the rate of opening are: the temperature of the drying environment, the time of day when the bud is picked and the moisture content of the stem. The less moisture the flower has, the less it will open up.

Most often *Helichrysum* flowers are mounted on wire. The head is picked and then a thin wire (usually 20 or 18 gauge) is pushed through the remnants of the stem. As the stem dries, it shrinks around the wire. The reason that one would choose to wire *Helichrysum* blossoms is that the stem is hygroscopic. When exposed to humidity, the weight of the blossom would make it droop. Another reason for wiring the flower has to do with the production of the plant. If only one flower is picked, then the rest of

the flower buds produce flowers.

Our choice is to pick the flowers on their own stems. Leaves are stripped and the bunch is hung up to dry. In picking the stem, the plant's production is reduced because the potential buds never have a chance to develop. On the other hand, flowers of *Helichrysum* are usually clustered; there are two or three buds just under the tip flower. If these are picked together with the stem, they dry in a group, conveying a more natural appearance as flowers rather than flower heads on wire stems.

Helipterum humboldtianum
HELIPTERUM

COMMON NAME: helipterum.
HISTORY: *Helipterum* comprises 60 to 90 annual or perennial herbs, subshrubs and shrubs native to South Africa, Australia and Tasmania. *H. humboldtianum* is a native of Western Australia. The outer bracts are brownish; the inner ones are pale lemon yellow. The plant is insignificant in stature, growing sparsely at first, producing large heads, an inch and a half across, and subsequently producing ones that are minute, a quarter inch across. The genus name is from the Greek *heli*, sun, and *pteron*, wing.

CULTIVATION: Seeds of *Helipterum* are approximately one-eighth inch long and the coat is hairy. They germinate readily and grow quickly. Unfortunately, plants are very fragile when transplanted and many die of shock even when individually potted. The plants quickly get exhausted in flower production. Even when constantly picked, the later smaller flower heads remain inconsequential. The merit of the plant is in its unique lemony color and shiny appearance.

PICKING: The flower stays exactly as picked—that is, it does not continue to develop very much. It should be picked when the whole head cluster is open flat. The side clusters will remain undeveloped.

Helipterum manglesii
RHODANTHE

COMMON NAMES: rhodanthe, Swan River Everlasting.
HISTORY: This is a branched plant with solitary white or pink flower heads on long peduncles. Originating in western Australia, the cultivar *maculatum* is a bit taller and has a flower with a wider range of pinkish colors.
CULTIVATION: See *H. humboldtianum*.
PICKING: Resembling *H. humboldtianum* in its manner, *H. manglesii* is also a plant of diminishing

returns—producing flowers that are successively smaller and smaller. Flowers on the stem are all at different stages of development, limiting its production potential and making picking tedious. Each flower can be cut with, at best, a four-inch stem. However, it is a plant definitely worth growing because of its coloration. The outside petals are a subtle delicate pink and the calyx is iridescent silver in appearance. The center is a dull grayish yellow. In contrast to *H. roseum*, rhodanthe is a more versatile flower to use in wreaths and arrangements.

Helipterum roseum
ACROCLINIUM

COMMON NAME: acroclinium.
HISTORY: A close relative of the preceding members of the genus, *H. roseum* is much more popular for dried-flower growing. It is easy to cultivate and is much more productive. It has centers that vary in color. Three kinds of centers appear interchangeably with white, pink and rose bracts—yellow, black with a yellow circle and totally black.

CULTIVATION: *H. roseum* is more malleable in the field than either of its close relatives. In transplanting, it does not suffer shock, and it grows quickly and produces readily. It is only toward the end of the summer that it begins to look tired. It should not be seeded too early, because quick growth results in a leggy and delicate plant that is more difficult to transplant into the field.
PICKING: This is an unusual flower in that it is very much affected by humidity and light in the way it opens and closes. Early in the morning or during wet weather, the flower is closed, resembling a bud. When the sun comes out and dries the surface of the petals, the flower opens fully. Even after the flower is picked in the late bud stage, it will keep on repeating this performance. For years after it has been dried, when days are humid, the flower will partially close. During dry winter months, the flower will open fully. Do not be alarmed by the flower's opening and closing. It has a life of its own and there is little that can be done to alter its behavior. Although acroclinium is easy to grow and stunning by itself, we find it difficult to use well in arrangements because of its brightness.

Limonium bonduellii
and *L. sinuatum*
STATICE

COMMON NAMES: statice, marsh rosemary, leadwort.
HISTORY: There are about 150 species of *Limonium;* most are perennial herbs that appear throughout the world. *L. bonduellii* and *L. sinuatum*, although two distinct species, are often listed together. However, *L. bonduellii*, which is

native to Algeria, differs from *L. sinuata* (native to the Mediterranean) in color; *L. bonduellii* is yellow whereas *L. sinuata* ranges from white to purple. In morphology, the two differ as well; the funnelform corolla of *L. bonduellii* is yellow and spur-like on the end, and the stem is tubular rather than winged or flat like that of *L. sinuata*. The name *Limonium* comes from the Greek *leimon*, meadow, in allusion to its common habitat.
CULTIVATION: *Limonium* species have a common habit of performing well in most moist soils. However, the plants do not like crowded or humid and cold conditions; leaves die back and the plant may rot at the crown. Seeds for common varieties of *Limonium* are sold by most seed houses in a decorticated form (without hulls). Apricot varieties are sometimes sold in hulls. All germinate well at room temperatures. The seed-

lings grow quickly and require little care beyond normal attention. The yellow species is quite susceptible to a fungus which settles on the calyx of the flower and takes the moisture out of the bud. Consequently, the flower never opens up and goes by without showing color. *Limonium* may not flower during long stretches of dark weather. Its best performance is during dry, sunny summers. In the fall, these plants fare well and can withstand the first light frosts.

PICKING: One should regard *L. sinuata* as a spike flower and pick it when approximately four-fifths of the head is developed. If there are any immature flowering side

branches on the stem, leave them for the next picking. After the stem is picked, the flowers tend to open a bit in drying. Various colors respond differently in drying and in the degree of opening. White, rose and apricot may have bottom flowers go by before the

top flowers open, or the flowers may not open at all. Most cleistogamous plants (those whose flowers do not open) seem to be from the population of these unusual colors.

The easiest colors to pick are the blues and violets (though the true blue colors are few and far

between). These colors grow on more rugged plants, have lots of moisture in the stem and open more after they are picked. The degree of flower opening and drying also varies with the amount of moisture in the stem. If the soil is dry, the flowers may open less. If the soil is moist, the flowers may

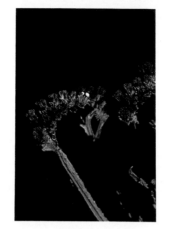

open more. When the flowers are reluctant to open after picking, or when you want to have a greater degree of control over the extent to which a flower opens, try picking a bit earlier and putting the stems in warm water for a few days. If the stem sears (as with cut flowers), further development of the blossom will cease. At that point, either renew the stem by trimming the seared part or pick the stems out of the bucket and hang the flowers upside down to dry.

Lonas annua
GOLDEN AGERATUM

COMMON NAMES: golden ageratum, African daisy, yellow ageratum.

HISTORY: Only one species exists of this annual herb that is native to the Mediterranean. The derivation of the genus name is unknown.

CULTIVATION: *Lonas* is easily started from seed. It requires no

special care and transplants easily into the field.

PICKING: *Lonas* is a plant of diminishing flowers. As the season progresses, flowers get smaller and smaller. The first flowers are up to two inches across. Subsequent flowers may consist of a cluster of one, making picking tedious. Toward the end of the season, the best thing to do is to cut the whole plant down to the ground and hang it up to dry. The flower cluster matures uniformly, unlike ageratum (to which it is not closely related). Pick when the whole cluster is open and uniformly golden.

Moluccella laevis
BELLS OF IRELAND

COMMON NAMES: bells of Ireland, Molucca balm, shellflower.

HISTORY: This curious plant, which is grown for its green smooth calyx shaped like a bell, got its genus name from the region where it was first found, the

Moluccas in the East Indies. *Laevis* means smooth. The plant itself has a faint lemony, minty aroma which remains with the plant after it has been dried.

CULTIVATION: *M. laevis* is propagated by seed. It germinates unevenly and over a long period of time. Unlike other large seeds, which should be covered for germinating, *Moluccella* seeds should merely be pressed into the surface of the medium and exposed to light. Transplanting is also unpredictable. Once the plant gets a start, it seems to thrive in moist rich soil and produces branches of spikes which often reach a height of three feet.

PICKING: Before the spikes start falling under their own weight, they should be cut and hung to dry. Because the green color is delicate, it should not be exposed to strong light. Eventually, the green becomes creamy. This is a curious plant in that it is far more attractive when it is in the field than when it is dried, for, even with the most delicate handling, the little bells readily fall off.

Nicandra physalodes
NICANDRA

COMMON NAMES: nicandra, apple-of-Peru, shoo-fly plant.

HISTORY: The genus name commemorates Nicander of Colophon, a poet who wrote about plants and their medicinal uses c. 100 B.C. Pods of Nicandra resemble pods of *Physalis* and husk tomatoes. The first of the common names refers to its place of origin; the second, to the reputed ability of the plant to repel white flies (something I have not had an opportunity to observe). Although there is only one species in this genus, the cultivar *violaceae* produces violet-blue flowers on top and white on the bottom half of the plant.

CULTIVATION: The plant is easily started from seed, like its relatives, the tomatoes. In fact, it sometimes becomes weedy. Although it is a delicate annual, it transplants easily and grows quickly. Its blue flowers would make it a worthwhile plant for the background garden even if it were not a plant grown for drying.

PICKING: If the pods, on their short stems, are picked constantly, the plant bloom will be constant and prolific. If, however, the pods are allowed to mature, the blooms will diminish. Pods can be picked when they are young but firm or when they are mature and brownish. Eventually, the green color will become creamy anyway. By far the easiest thing to do is to pick the whole plant and use the pods as needed.

Nigella damascena
NIGELLA

COMMON NAMES: nigella, love-in-the-mist, wild fennel, love-in-a-puzzle, devil-in-a-bush, St. Catherine's flower, Persian jewels.

HISTORY: Most of the 20 species that exist are native to the Mediterranean and western Asia. The botanical names refer to the color of the seed and to the place of association, Damascus. The common name wild fennel is misleading, for fennel belongs to the

Umbelliferae family and is in no way a relative of *Nigella*.

CULTIVATION: *Nigella* seeds can easily be germinated at normal room temperature (you can save the seeds from overmature pods). However, *Nigella* does not like to be transplanted. The delicate roots can be injured very easily. In transplanting, one must also be careful not to bury the crown leaves. The transplanted seedling may sit immobile for many days, and only when the weather gets warm will it start moving along and putting on shoots and flowers.

PICKING: *Nigella* is a beautiful plant. It has flowers that are blue or white, delicate and distinctive. Although the flower petals shrivel when dried, they are still attractive because they retain the delicate fennel-like leaves and color. The pods should be picked when a burgundy cast appears between the pod lobes. If pods are allowed

to go for much longer without being picked, they will turn dull brown, split and become extremely fragile. At that point, the pod is more useful for its contents—the seeds—than for its decorative value.

Ocimum basilicum
and Ocimum spp.
BASIL

COMMON NAMES: common basil, sweet basil; also varieties including lemon basil, opal basil and cinnamon basil; as well as species O. kilimandjaricum (camphor basil) and O. sanctum (holy basil).

HISTORY: The genus name is derived from the Greek okimon, to smell: strong-smelling. Various species names refer to their geographical origins, characteristics or ritual uses. For instance, O. sanctum is a ritual plant in the Vedic religion. O. basilicum has been variously associated with sanctity or the devil. In all, there are over 150 Ocimum species of herbs and shrubs which inhabit the warm regions of Asia, the Mediterranean and Africa.

CULTIVATION: This tender annual should be started indoors. Opal and lemon basil varieties are fairly finicky. Although easy to germinate, they are sensitive to soil

Ocimum basilicum   O. sanctum

O. basilicum var. cinnamon

moisture. Once in the field, they should be allowed enough space for air to penetrate and dry the moisture off the leaves because during humid weather flowers, leaves, and often stems are susceptible to mildew or fungus. Basils scent the evening air with a licorice aroma, making them desirable garden plants even if there were no other uses.

PICKING: For decorative purposes, it is the plant's spike that is used. It is woven into wreaths or used subtly in arrangements. Basil retains fragrance very well. Unfortunately, the leaves are fragile; the spike is less so. Picking should be done when the weather is dry—preferably at midday, after the sun has dried the dew off the flowers. Both long and short spikes can be utilized.

Psylliostachys suworowii
RUSSIAN STATICE

COMMON NAMES: Russian statice, rat-tail statice.

HISTORY: This is one of seven or eight species of plants that are native to the southern regions of the Soviet Union, the Caucasus, Afghanistan and Israel. It is an unusual plant that is not readily available through catalogues. Seeds are also fairly rare. Its spike

is pink and slightly sweet-smelling.

CULTIVATION: The germination rate is poor. Less than half of all seeds germinate even if given ideal conditions—bottom heat and plenty of humidity. Growth is slow, and the plant seems to walk a tightrope between sufficient moisture to grow well and to resist spider-mite damage, on the one hand, and damping-off from excess moisture in the soil, on the

other. When transplanting, watch out for damage to the roots; they are delicate.

PICKING: Spikes bloom from the bottom up. When the spike is approximately two-thirds developed, it should be cut. There will be other side shoots developing, but they will not be as large as the first one.

Ratibida columnifera
RATIBIDA

COMMON NAMES: ratibida, Mexican hat plant, prairie coneflower.

HISTORY: In this genus there are five species of North American annual and perennial herbs. Like its close relative Rudbeckia (where it was once classified), this species blooms the first year. The variety pulcherrima is a double-flowered form which is useful as a cut flower. The species name refers

to the shape of the pod, which is column-like.

CULTIVATION: The seeds of this daisy plant are fairly fine. It is important to have a low density of germinating seedlings. *Ratibida* transplants well and grows quickly, producing a multitude of interesting, if unspectacular, flowers.

PICKING: Pods should be picked shortly after the flower ray petals fall off. Or the pods can be picked with the petals. The petals, however, shrink and do not contribute much to the shape of the pod.

Salvia farinacea
BLUE SALVIA

COMMON NAMES: blue salvia, mealy-cup sage.
HISTORY: *S. farinacea* is native to New Mexico and Texas and is one of 750 species of *Salvia*.

While most books list this as a perennial, it really should be treated as an annual. The variety alba has a white spike. The genus name is associated with *salvus*, safe, well, sound—a property attributed to other salvias that were used medicinally. The species name refers to the mealy form of the flower. This is an unusual flower for drying. When in the garden, there is a purplish cast to the flower. Once hung up to dry, it will become blue, losing its reddish color component. The blue color is true in its blueness while also unique in tone.

CULTIVATION: Seeds of *S. farinacea* germinate quickly at room temperature. A curious thing happens to the seeds of many members of the Labiatae family. The seed, once watered, soon comes to look like an eyeball—the outer seed sheath absorbs water and gets a whitish gelatinously slippery appearance. *Salvia* and other Labiatae seeds (especially lavender and rosemary) germinate better when sown on the surface of the soil and provided with ample moisture and light. Once the seeds germinate, the surface of the soil should be kept on the dry side in order to prevent damping-off. Another curiosity about *S. farinacea* is the odor of its foliage (but, luckily, not that of its flowers), which resembles the scent left by a male cat.

In the garden, *Salvia* prefers rich soil and full sun. It is tolerant to dryness but will not produce as many flowers under dry conditions.

PICKING: The *Salvia* spike varies in size from the beginning to the end of the season. At the beginning, it may approach six inches; at the end, only two or three. It all depends on the amount of moisture in the soil and the tempera-

ture of the air. *Salvia* should be picked when approximately four-fifths of the spike is developed. Because the spike production is generally such that at the bottom of the stem two more side spikes are forming, the spike that is to be picked will be approximately six inches. The stem is tinged blue and is square. A word of caution: *S. farinacea* has to be tied in small bunches and placed in an airy dry spot. It will mildew readily if there is too much humidity.

Salvia splendens and ×*superba*
SALVIA

COMMON NAMES: salvia, scarlet sage.
HISTORY: There are many cultivars of *S. splendens*, including *alba* (white), *atropurpurea* (purplish), *atrosanguinea* (dark crimson). The most familiar color of scarlet sage is the red; however, there are many colors and forms, including dwarf and tall varieties. It is a perennial from Brazil but is grown primarily as an annual. The color is so vibrant that the species name *splendens* implies that it is splendid for gardens.

CULTIVATION: In most cases, similar conditions are required for *S. splendens*, *S.* × *superba* and *S. farinacea*. One difference is that the former are more delicate plants and cannot tolerate cold. Another difference, of course, is that the hybrids produce sterile seed or no seed at all.

PICKING: Picking these large-flowered specimens is tricky. Spikes should be picked when they are two-thirds to four-fifths developed. They should be dried rather quickly because they are full of moisture and have a tendency to lose flowers at the bottom of the spike and to mildew in the center if the drying period is extended.

Salvia viridis
SALVIA

COMMON NAME: salvia.
HISTORY: This is a very unusual plant originating in Southern Europe. It comes in white, pink and violet. But the terminal bracts are

similar in form to Poinsettia where color appears on leaves at the tips of branches. The terminal bracts are sterile flowers; the calyx is tubular and small, located well below the top of the plant. We surmise that the color of the terminal bracts attracts pollinating insects. This salvia is an attractive and long-lasting cut flower as well.
CULTIVATION: *S. viridis* is hardy and persistent. It will often re-

seed itself from one year to another. In the greenhouse, it should not be started too early because it will fill its pot very quickly, rapidly absorbing the available moisture and subsequently wilting in the sun.
PICKING: Pick all through the summer when the quality of the bloom is at its peak and when more of the stem is colored. When the seed production increases, the quality of color deteriorates. Overall, it is a pleasant everlasting. Although the bracts shrivel a bit, the drying process is simple and the color retention is good.

Scabiosa stellata
SCABIOSA

COMMON NAMES: scabiosa, star flower, paper moon.
HISTORY: In this genus there are over 80 species of annual and perennial herbs native to Europe, Asia and Africa. The Burpee seed company introduced it to the United States a few years ago.

Scabiosa stellata flower

This plant is native to the western Mediterranean region. It derives its genus name from the Latin meaning to itch, for which *Scabiosus* was used as a cure. *Stellata* means star-like.
CULTIVATION: The starry seed pods are composed of a number of seeds that resemble badminton shuttlecocks around a hollow center. Seeds germinate quickly and are very hardy, but the plants

grow rapidly, and if they are started too early in the spring, they will get leggy and become difficult to transplant. The roots are limited and any minute damage to the system may kill the plant. First blooms come quickly. Subsequent ones are prolific—

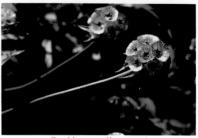

Scabiosa stellata pod

that is, until the plant becomes tired of producing flowers and finally succumbs to old age.
PICKING: The pods should be picked just when the stars inside the "shuttlecocks" start turning from green to black. This is the time when they are largest. Any delay in picking will result in a pod that shatters too readily. The stem on which the pod is suspended is quite fibrous, so it has to be cut with shears or clippers.

Tagetes erecta
MARIGOLD

COMMON NAMES: marigold, African marigold, Aztec marigold.
HISTORY: There are about 30 spe-

cies of marigolds which are native from Arizona and New Mexico to Argentina. *T. erecta* and *T. patula* (French marigold) are native to Mexico and Central America but are now spread widely throughout the warm regions, where they are used as ornamentals and cut flowers.

CULTIVATION: Marigolds are prolifically flowering plants when given adequate moisture and rich, warm soil. Seeded in the greenhouse in March, they should be transplanted after any danger of frost has passed, since they are not at all frost-hardy.

PICKING: Marigolds are not true dry flowers. They are full of moisture and, if dried slowly, most often rot right on the stem. They should be picked just before maturity—before the calyx has split due to the force of growing seeds. As soon as flowers are picked, they should be hung to dry in a very warm dry area with adequate ventilation. In drying, the flowers shrink to about a half of their original size. For that reason, the smaller French marigolds are really not suitable for drying.

Xeranthemum annuum
XERANTHEMUM

COMMON NAMES: xeranthemum, immortelle.

HISTORY: This is one of the oldest-known everlastings native to Southern Europe. There are six species in the genus, of which *X. annuum* is the most popular. The flowers come in white, pink and rose, but even those that turn brownish when gone by, retain their shape and are attractive. The name *Xeranthemum* comes from the Greek *xeros*, dry, and *anthos*, flower.

CULTIVATION: *Xeranthemum* is easily propagated by seed. The seeds germinate readily and the plant grows quickly. However, *Xeranthemum* has a delicate root system. Roots should be separated carefully and the plant should not be handled roughly in

the garden. Although the plant is versatile in its soil demands, it needs moisture (but not wet feet) to be truly productive.

PICKING: *Xeranthemum* flowers stay exactly as you pick them. They do not open or close. The petals, however, are very fragile and will bend if placed on the ground. You should make small bunches, which should be placed standing on the stems in a container or hung up immediately. If the flower petals bend under their own weight, it is unlikely that they will straighten in drying. Also, the fibrous stem requires that the flowers be cut with shears. Any tugging on the plant and its roots may result in serious injury.

Gardener's Guide for Annual Everlastings

PAGE NUMBER	GENUS	SPECIES	COMMON NAME	HEIGHT	PLANTING DISTANCE	PART USED
44	Abutilon	theophrasti	velvet leaf	5′	5′	pod
44–45	Ageratum	houstonianum	ageratum, bedding type	10″	10″	flower
44–45	Ageratum	houstonianum	ageratum, tall	3′	3′	flower
47	Agrostis	spp.	cloud grass	12″	12″	flower
45	Amaranthus	caudatus	amaranthus	24″	24″	flower
43, 46	Ammobium	alatum	ammobium	2′	12″	flower
46	Artemisia	annua	sweet wormwood	6′	2′	plant
47	Avena	sterilis	animated oats	3′	12″	flower
47	Briza	maxima	quaking grass	2′	12″	flower
47–48	Calendula	officinalis	calendula	18″	12″	flower
48	Cardiospermum	halicacabum	love-in-a-puff	10′	12″	pod
48–49	Carthamus	tinctorius	safflower	30″	18″	flower
43, 49	Celosia	argentea	cockscomb	2′	12″	flower
49	Celosia	argentea	plumed celosia	2′	18″	flower
43, 49–52	Centaurea	cyanus	bachelor's button	2′	18″	flower
52	Chenopodium	botrys	ambrosia	18″	12″	plant
52–53	Chrysanthemum	ptarmiciflorum	dusty miller	12″	12″	foliage
47	Coix	lacryma	Job's tears	3′	12″	flower
53	Consolida	ambigua	larkspur	2′	12″	flower
53–56	Cotula	barbata	pincushion plant	5″	3″	flower
56	Emilia	javanica	tassel flower	24″	12″	flower
47	Eragrostis	spp.	love grass	2′	12″	flower
56	Eucalyptus	cinerea	eucalyptus	3′	18″	foliage
44, 56–57	Gomphrena	globosa	globe amaranth	24″	18″	flower
44, 56–57	Gomphrena	haageana	orange globe amaranth	18″	18″	flower
57	Helichrysum	angustifolium	golden baby	12″	12″	flower
57	Helichrysum	arenarium	dwarf yellow immortelle	12″	12″	flower
44, 57–58	Helichrysum	bracteatum	strawflower	4′	2′	flower
57	Helichrysum	orientale	golden mothwort	12″	12″	flower
57	Helichrysum	stoechas	golden Cassidony	12″	12″	flower
57	Helichrysum	thianschanicum	curry plant	12″	12″	flower
58	Helipterum	humboldtianum	helipterum	18″	6″	flower
44, 58–59	Helipterum	manglesii	rhodanthe	18″	6″	flower
44, 59	Helipterum	roseum	acroclinium	20″	12″	flower
44, 59–60	Limonium	bonduellii	statice	3′	18″	flower
44, 59–60	Limonium	sinuatum	statice	3′	18″	flower
60	Lonas	annua	golden ageratum	12″	12″	flower
60–61	Moluccella	laevis	bells of Ireland	3′	18″	flower
61	Nicandra	physalodes	nicandra	5′	3′	pods
61–62	Nigella	damascena	nigella	18″	18″	flower and pod
62	Ocimum	basilicum	basil	3′	2′	flower
62	Ocimum	kilimandjaricum	camphor basil	3′	2′	flower
62	Ocimum	sanctum	holy basil	3′	2′	flower
62	Psylliostachys	suworowii	Russian statice	12″	10″	flower
62, 63	Ratibida	columnifera	ratibida	3′	2′	pod
43, 63	Salvia	farinacea	blue salvia	3′	2′	flower
43, 63–64	Salvia	splendens	salvia	2′	18″	flower
64	Salvia	viridis	salvia	2′	18″	terminal bract
64	Scabiosa	stellata	scabiosa	12″	12″	pod
47	Secale	spp.	rye	3′	12″	flower
47	Setaria	italica	foxtail	3′	12″	flower
47	Stipa	spp.	feather grass	3′	12″	flower
64–65	Tagetes	erecta	marigold	3′	3′	flower
47	Triticum	spp.	wheat	3′	12″	flower
43, 65	Xeranthemum	annuum	xeranthemum	18″	18″	flower

Amaranthus candatus

4

Perennials

Growing perennials is
rewarding, if for nothing else than the
plants' longevity. Perennials come back year
after year, and in their persistence they evoke
a concern that makes them long-lasting friends.
Contrary to common belief, perennials are not
plants that care for themselves. Because they live in
one spot for an extended period of time, they need special
attention. For instance, the soil must be carefully prepared.
Nutrients must be regularly replenished, but only during limited
intervals—between spring and the end of July. Perennials must be
marked for identification so that a zealous weeder in the spring does
not confuse desirable with undesirable plants. By the same

token, some perennials become weedy and must be restrained from taking over the whole garden.

There is pleasure in growing perennials for their diversity and multiplicity of uses. For decoration, some perennials are excellent both as cut and dried flowers. Some are used medicinally. Others are valued for their culinary uses and for their fragrance. Certain species are known for their insecticidal and insect-repelling properties.

In general, perennial plants that are useful as everlastings are less showy than annual plants. Once dry, they do tend to have subdued colors and tones that are less emphatic than those of annuals such as blue salvia (*Salvia farinacea*) or strawflower (*Helichrysum bracteatum*). In fact, this is not a negative characteristic, for perennials produce either foliage, pods, or flowers that allow the designer to form, shape and define backgrounds that emphasize the accents created with annual everlastings. Where else but from perennials, growing in the wild or in a cultivated garden, would the designer be able to get enough filler material? *Artemisia, Solidago, Achillea, Gypsophila* and others are the background of most designs and are the essential constituent of every garden that is designed for the production of everlastings.

Many plants listed in this section have long histories of use among varied populations in diverse parts of the world. The longer a plant is grown, the greater the number of names it acquires and the more complex are the legends surrounding it. On the other hand, some plants in this section are recent introductions. Their existence is new in the world of plants. They are the result of human manipulation, of

breeding. Consequently, they are known only in their hybrid forms.

Achillea filipendulina
GOLDEN YARROW

COMMON NAMES: golden yarrow, fern-leafy yarrow, yellow yarrow.
HISTORY: Most of the 60 to 100 species of *Achillea* are native to the Old World. Some have naturalized in the temperate zones of North America. *A. filipendulina*

(meaning fern-like) is native to Asia Minor and the Caucasus. The genus is named after Achilles, the heroic figure in the wars between Greece and Troy. It is said that he used this plant to treat his soldiers' wounds. The common name yarrow comes from the Anglo-Saxon *gearwe*. The leaves have a peculiar resinous, medicinal fragrance that reminds one of a hospital.
CULTIVATION: Curiously, it seems to be more prone to disease than any of the other *Achillea* species; for example, it is the only one that

sustains substantial damage from the tarnished plant bug (*Lygus lineolaris*). The bug's toxin causes the bud either to become deformed or to turn brown. This bug is difficult to eradicate because it crawls under the head of the flower when it senses any motion; therefore, any spray directed at the bug is ineffective unless systemic insecticides are used (we would not recommend that method). To keep the bugs at bay, keep the area around the plants free of weeds; insects overwinter in overgrown areas.

Unlike *A. millefolium* and the cultivar *rosea*, which bloom from seed the first year, *A. filipendulina* will bloom in the second year. It is also a delicate plant to transplant. The roots are fairly deep, and after *Achillea* is dug up, it wilts, requiring several weeks to recover completely.
PICKING: Flower heads should be picked when the individual flowers are completely open—when the inner and outer rays are completely flat. If the flowers are picked too early, they will shrink in such a way that the brilliant yellow color will not show. If picked too late, the center will bulge up and the outside petals of individual flowers will fall off. The color will become brownish.

Achillea millefolium
YARROW

COMMON NAMES: common yarrow, milfoil, woundwort, staunchgrass, bloodwort, soldier's woundwort, nosebleed, sanguinary, thousand-seal, carpenter's weed.
HISTORY: Although native to Europe, it is widespread in temperate regions of North America, where it has become naturalized. It is now prolific in dry soil, along

roads and fields. Propagated by seed or root division, this is a hardy perennial yarrow with lacy white heads. Paiute Indians apparently used it for stomach disorders. Calling it by the name of

squirreltail, Winnebago and Chippewa Indians used it medicinally for headache. Linnaeus also mentions its use in brewing beer—to make the brew a more powerful intoxicant. Though dismissed from the U.S. Pharmacopoeia, it is still used in folk medicine (as well as for I Ching sticks). The common name milfoil comes from the Norman-French *mille-feuille*, fine-cut leaves.

CULTIVATION: Cultivated before the mid-fifteenth century, *A. millefolium* is distinguished by being allelopathic to itself. That is, in poor soil, within a period of two to three years this plant will die out because it produces a toxin that is poisonous to itself. At first, upon reading about this phenomenon in respect to *Achillea*, we were very skeptical because ours, in rich garden soil, grew in the same spot for several years. But eventually, it also died out. We have observed the same process in the wild, where, most often, white daisies take over the area after *A. millefolium*. Thus, every year we have to look for a new patch in the wild to supplement our home-grown. We have not observed the

same phenomenon with other *Achillea* species.

PICKING: The same rules apply for drying *A. millefolium* as for drying *A. filipendulina*. The time of picking in the wild on dry terrain, however, is critical, because what little moisture there is in the plant goes into development of the flower. At a certain point, the flower will go by rapidly.

Achillea millefolium var. *rosea* ROSE YARROW

COMMON NAME: rose or red yarrow.

HISTORY: The cultivar is a three-foot plant with a morphology similar to that of *A. millefolium*. The cultivar Cerise Queen, which is found in western North America, ranges from light pink to rose

color. In our area we have never observed any wild *A. millefolium* that was any darker than a light shade of pink. In England, the red form was discovered by Gerard.

CULTIVATION: *A. millefolium* and Cv. *rosea* should be divided often, for they consume soil nutrition rapidly. Divide in the spring before leaves are well developed.

PICKING: Although the cultivar *rosea* does not dry true to the bright beautiful color that is so stunning when it is fresh, it is nevertheless quite useful in combination with other muted blos-

soms—such as those of oregano. When dry, the texture of this flower resembles that of a delicate old lace.

Achillea ptarmica THE PEARL

COMMON NAMES: the pearl, shirt-buttons, goosetongue, sneeze-wort, sneezeweed.

HISTORY: This yarrow is sometimes referred to as sneezewort because, dried and powdered, it was used as snuff. Gerard referred to a double *Ptarmica* as *P. duplici-flore* and called another plant, *P. austriaca*, sneezewort of Austrich; other names mentioned by Gerard are *Pyrethrum sylvestre*, *Draco sylvestris* or *Tarcon sylvestris*, *Sternut amentoria* (because it caused sneezing), *Tanacetum acutum album* and, in English, wild Pellitorie (a name describing a sharp and biting taste). It is a plant that in structure is unlike any of the preceding *Achillea* species: the flower is single. People who have

not worked with *A. ptarmica* often confuse it with *Chrysanthemum parthenium*, feverfew. In fact, the flower is more like that of a double feverfew than the flowers of the preceding *Achillea* species. Its single flower is an enormous magnification of one flower from an *A. millefolium* cluster. The leaves are also unlike those of *A. millefolium* or *Matricaria;* they are single, slender and a duller green, without a pungent aroma. This plant also resembles, in its airiness, a fairly large-bloomed *Gypsophila.* Cultivated by the end of the sixteenth century, it was appreciated for its long-lasting blooms. In certain parts of rural England, it was carried by bridesmaids and called Seven Years' Love. Hilderic Friend noted that the double-flowered form was carried to the wedding altar by the bride. With its almost iridescent white, *A. ptarmica* probably signified purity and chastity.

CULTIVATION: It is propagated by seeds and root cuttings.

PICKING: Pick when the flower is developed but before the center starts losing its color. Unlike feverfew, dried *A. ptarmica* is as pure white as *Ammobium.*

Achillea tomentosa
Cv. *aurea*
WOOLLY YARROW

COMMON NAME: woolly yarrow.

HISTORY: This plant is a miniature version of *A. filipendulina;* however, the individual flowers in a cluster are larger. The plant is of European and western Asian origin. It is used primarily as a decorative plant in gardens, blooming in May and June.

CULTIVATION: See preceding *Achillea* species.

PICKING: *A. tomentosa* produces blooms not unlike those of *A. filipendulina.* However, when picked to dry, the blossom is more airy—not tight-clustered. Pick when all the individual flowers are fully open.

Alchemilla vulgaris
LADY'S MANTLE

COMMON NAMES: lady's mantle, lion's foot.

HISTORY: There are about 200 species in this genus; they have basal green-gray foliage and flower stalks (in this species coming to a height of approximately eighteen inches). There are other, closely related species that are often found under the heading of *vulgaris. A. alpina* and *A. arvensis* are often mentioned in books. Mostly they are found in the north temperate zone. *Alchemilla* is an airy plant with panicles of flowers high above the base of the stem.

Apparently, the plant was not known by ancient writers. However, during the sixteenth century, alchemists, believing that dew had great curative powers, thought the plant was magical because it collected dew in its lobed leaves. The genus name is from *alkemelya,* of Arabic origin.

CULTIVATION: Propagated by seed or by root division, the plant prefers moist rich soil and will do well in full sun or partial shade. The seeds are fine: they should not be covered but, rather, pressed lightly into the soil. *Alchemilla* will last long in the perennial garden, requiring little care or attention since it is not particularly susceptible to insect attacks. The only thing to watch for is crown rot in the cool months of spring, caused by too much moisture around the basal cluster. Plant it on a well-drained raised bed to prevent this problem. The plant flowers from seed in the second year. It blooms from June through July or until the weather gets hot.

PICKING: The flower should be picked at the height of bloom. In its effect in arrangements it resembles *Limonium nashii* or *L. latifolium.* The color holds well.

Allium caeruleum, A. schoenoprasum and *Allium* spp.
ALLIUM

COMMON NAMES: onion, chive, leek, garlic, garlic chive.

HISTORY: *A. caeruleum* has chive-like blue blossoms on 12–18-inch stalks with 1–2-inch heads. Many *Allium* species can be dried, including *A. cepa* (onion—white bloom on stems up to 3 feet tall), *A. ampeloprasum* (leek—light pink to purplish bloom on stems up to 5 feet tall), *A. schoenoprasum* (chive—pink and deep lavender blooms up to 2 feet tall) and *A. tuberosum* (garlic chive or Chinese chive) (white blooms on stems 18 inches tall). Onions and onion cultivars have been under cultivation since the dawn of civilization. They are mentioned by Chaldeans, Egyptians and Greeks. In A.D. 42, Columella used the word

Allium tuberosum ▴   ▾ *Allium schoenoprasum*

Allium ampeloprasum

Allium cepa

unionem, which gave rise to our common name onion. Chives are native to Europe but are found naturalized in North America. Garlic was used by Egyptians and Romans to sustain the strength of their slaves.

There are more than 400 species of *Allium*. When bruised, many are strongly scented. They have been used in cooking, medicine and decoration. *Allium* comes from the Celtic *all*, meaning hot or pungent. Garlic was thought to be a remedy for every disease or body malfunction. The common name garlic comes from the Anglo-Saxon *gar*, a lance (stem), and *leac*, a potherb. In fact, it is now known that the oils of onion and garlic have many vitamins, including A, B_1, B_2 and C, as well as antibacterial agents. Also, garlic is utilized in the treatment of hypertension and arteriosclerosis.

CULTIVATION: Alliums like moist, warm rich soil. They generally bloom the second year when started from seed. Most fresh seeds germinate readily and require no special care. However, to germinate, the seed coat should have sufficient moisture. In order to maintain good-quality blooms, bulb clumps should be divided periodically; once every two years is sufficient. If onion chives are

cut down after the spring bloom, they will bloom again in the fall months, but not in profusion.

PICKING: Flowers should be picked just after the top tubules on the blossoms open and then should be dried immediately. If the flowers are picked much later, the seeds will begin to develop and the flowers will lose color and become shaggy. The stems of chives, leeks and onions will keep green for as long as seed production continues. For a long time after the stem is picked, the stem stays green and the flower attempts to eke out a seed. If the flower is picked sufficiently early, no seed production takes place. However, do not be concerned if drying takes a long time. If provided with sufficient air circulation, *Allium* will dry without any problems.

Anaphalis margaritacea
PEARLY EVERLASTING

COMMON NAMES: pearly everlasting, cad-weed, rabbit-tobacco, silver-leaf, life everlasting, cotton weed, none so pretty, moonshine, Indian posy, ladies' tobacco, poverty weed, silver button.

HISTORY: It is found wild in mountainous temperate regions of North America and eastern Asia.

There are approximately 35 species, with primarily *A. margaritacea* in cultivation. According to Gerard, Clusius called it *Gnaphalium americanum* after obtaining a sample from England (it is speculated that Raleigh may have brought it from Virginia).

Anaphalis was used instead of tobacco and was thought to possess the virtues of cleaning lungs, abating coughs and alleviating the pain of headaches. Medicinally, American Indians also used the plant described variously as *G. polycephalum*, *G. obtusifolium* (see Chapter 5) or *A. margaritacea*.

Montagnais used decoctions for coughing, consumption and stomach sickness. Mohegans used it for making teas in the treatment of colds. Cheyennes dropped the plant on hot coals; they believed that it had a purifying effect, and before battles they rubbed the herb over their bodies to provide strength and energy. In combination with wild mint, Chippewas used it in rituals for curing paralysis. Menominis, Ojibwas, Potawatomis and Mohawks also used the plant in rituals and medicinally.

CULTIVATION: *A. margaritacea* grows to three feet high in rich soil. In the wild, it will be found in dry wastelands. This plant spreads rapidly, requiring occasional thinning. Thinning is also necessary because under certain humid conditions—with little wind—it may mildew and rot. It is also possible to propagate *Anaphalis* by seed. In the greenhouse, as outside, seedlings should not be overwatered. *Anaphalis* attracts a painted lady moth (*Vanessa virginiensis*), caterpillars of which damage buds, leaves and flowers. If *Anaphalis* is planted next to *Artemisia*, this moth will invade the tips of *Artemisia* (perhaps being confused by the similarity in color). The damage to *Artemisia* may be substantial and much more costly because it is not as prolific as *Anaphalis*. Although a useful everlasting, *Anaphalis* is not as valuable as *Artemisia* in wreath making or arranging.

PICKING: The flower head, which is very similar to that of *Gnaphalium*, should be picked before it opens—that is, when the bud is large but still tight. All is not lost, however, if you pick it late. The center will puff out and the prominent seed will eventually fall out as in a dandelion. If the seed does not drop out, you can beat the flowers lightly against your leg to release the seed. What you will have left will be white starry petals—still attractive in arrangements.

Aquilegia × hybrida
COLUMBINE

COMMON NAMES: columbine, European crowfoot, garden crowfoot.

HISTORY: *Aquilegia canadensis*, one of about 70 species inhabiting north temperate zones, used to be quite prolific in the wild. Now it is a protected species. *A. canadensis* and many of its relatives, such as *A. caerulea* (called by Gerard *Herba leonis*, herb in which the lion does delight), according

to Coats was introduced to England from the Rocky Mountains in 1864. *A. vulgaris*, *A. chrysantha* (introduced from California in 1873) and possibly other species contributed to producing the now popular long-spurred hybrid varieties. The first useful spurred variety was grown by Douglas, a florist in England at the end of the nineteenth century.

It is one of the few plants which, according to Gerard, had little medicinal value but was planted, nevertheless, to decorate the gardens "of the curious" and to be used in garlands. When mentioned by Shakespeare in *Hamlet*, it was a symbol of the cuckold: "The blue cornuted columbine, Like to the crooked horns of Acheloy." Theories about the derivation of the genus name vary. According to some sources, it comes either from the Latin *aqua*, water, in reference to the environment in which it prefers to live, or from the Latin *aquila*, eagle, referring to the shape of the petals. One source suggests that both *aquila* and *columba*, dove, refer to the shape of the petals.

CULTIVATION: *Aquilegia* prefers moist soil and will survive in a moderately acid environment. It is easily propagated from seed, though the seed may be finicky in germinating. The best way to

handle the seed is to press it into the soil, cover it with glass and germinate quickly. Most often, blooms come in the second year.

PICKING: Pods are picked after they open up. Shake out the seed for some volunteers in the spring.

Armeria maritima
ARMERIA

COMMON NAMES: armeria, thrift, ladies' cushion, sea pink.

HISTORY: Research shows that this is a fairly polymorphic species with many geographic variations. Thus, it comes under many different names, in different sizes and shapes. In all, there are as many as 35 species of *Armeria*. Most seeds that are sold under different species names actually belong to the polymorphic *A. maritima*. They hybridize readily and are not easily distinguishable.

Although common names are sea pink or thrift, in Gerard's time Sweet Williams were called *Armeria*, and *Armeria* was also called Tolmeiners, London Tufts and Sia Gillofloure. It was found in sea marshes in England and in Northern Europe, and when Pliny classified it under the name statice, he implied that it stopped shifting dunes. Later sea lavender and statice, with which *Armeria* was originally classified, were

Aquilegia × *hybrida* McKana's Hybrids

Armeria maritima

placed in the genus *Limonium*. *Armeria* flowers are in a cluster; those of *Limonium sinuata* are in a spike.

Armeria was one of the first plants to be used in knot gardens when they became fashionable. But because they were variably winter-hardy, they required constant care and replanting. Even with such drawbacks, in both England and Holland they were popular edging plants.

CULTIVATION: From seed, *Armeria* will bloom the first year. It is propagated either by seed or by root division. A low-growing, fairly hardy perennial that prefers well-drained soil, *Armeria* produces some of the first blooms in the spring.

PICKING: The flower should be picked when it is almost completely open—as it opens a bit after being picked. If it is picked at the right time, its color, although not intense, will shade the flower head.

Artemisia absinthium
WORMWOOD

COMMON NAMES: common wormwood, absinthe, ware-moth.

HISTORY: There are more than 200 species of *Artemisia* throughout the Northern Hemisphere with a few in South America. The genus contains annual, biennial and perennial species of herbs and shrubs. Most of them are aromatic. Many species are highly variable with a tendency to cross readily. Many species have been used for medicine—*pontica, vulgaris, absinthium. A. drucunculus* (Russian tarragon) and *A. drucunculus* var. *sativa* (French tarragon) have been used extensively in cooking. Many are also popular decorative plants. Most thrive in poor soil (being resilient to drought) and are propagated by root or stem cuttings. Some, like *A. absinthium, vulgare, annua* and *genipi* (syn. *spicata*) are also propagated by seed.

Much confusion exists as to the fertility of the seed. Most sources say that French tarragon can only be propagated by root cuttings. The same thing applies to *A. ludoviciana* and Cv. *albula*, which is variously listed as Silver Queen or Silver King, both of which occur in the southern and southwestern United States. Existing confusion about the species and their identification is also caused by high intraspecies variability. For instance, leaves of *A. ludoviciana* vary from lanceolate to oval up to 4½ inches long.

A. ludoviciana leaves are fairly leathery and do not readily shatter in handling. *Absinthium, annua, vulgaris* and *schmidtiana* are fairly fragile. Though they are useful, they are delicate and require patience in handling. *A. stelleriana*, variously called beach artemisia or dusty miller (yet another plant by that common name), has wide leathery leaves that resemble those of *Senecio cineraria*, but are not prolific enough to be useful in design.

A. abrotanum (southernwood) has green foliage that is crumbly when dried. Native to the Old World, specifically found growing on the banks of the Volga River in Russia by John Tradescant, "God's Tree," as it was called, is heavily scented with a lemony fragrance.

Although *A. absinthium* is native to Southern Europe, it is now found wild in the eastern U.S. According to a legend, it originated in the tracks of the serpent in the Garden of Eden. Medicinally, it was used as a vermifuge. As a constituent of an alcoholic beverage, it was used by the Saracens and, until recently, by the French. Unfortunately, alkaloids in absinthe also have a tendency to cause deterioration of the nervous system, resulting in delirium and sometimes death. *A. pontica*, less objectionable in its results and in its strength, is used to flavor vermouth. In reference to its bitter qualities and ability to poison the soil, Ovid wrote: "Untilled barren ground the lothsome Wormwood yields, And knowne it's by the fruit how bitter are the fields."

According to some records, *Artemisia* is named after Artemisia, the wife of Mausolus, but the name existed before that and most probably the genus is named after Artemis, goddess of the moon, the hunt (and forest) and chastity, and the plants bearing her name

were so honored because of their medicinal virtues.

CULTIVATION: *A. absinthium* is one of the few valuable members of the genus that can be started readily from seed. Although the seed germinates readily, it should not be stored for more than two years, because its viability decreases. Another way to propagate the plant is by stem cuttings early in the spring. From seed, it blooms in the second year. However, we have found that since it is the foliage that is more important in providing bulk in wreath making, *A. absinthium* should either be cut early in the season or raised from seed every second year. Once the plant puts out spikes of inflorescence, it becomes woody and, consequently, less useful. Therefore, it is best to renew the plant periodically. A unique problem that may also be present with all *Artemisia* species is that they tend to be allelopathic—poisoning the soil for other cultivated delicate plants in their immediate vicinity.

PICKING: Picking should take place when the leaves are largest. On first-year plants this is usually done in late August; on older plants it may be done at the end of June. *A. absinthium* foliage is fairly moist. When it is harvested, it should be dried in an airy spot in order to avoid problems with mildew.

Artemisia
ludoviciana
ARTEMISIA

COMMON NAMES: artemisia, Silver King, Silver Queen, western wormwood, cudweed, white sage.
HISTORY: Native to the southwestern U.S., this has become a popular landscape plant. Because

it is variable in its form due to crossing with other species, photographs illustrating the species may vary from one source to another. The variety *albula*, native to northern Mexico, has foliage that is white tomentose on both surfaces. This feature makes it especially valuable in design because all colors contrast readily with grayish-white.

CULTIVATION: *A. ludoviciana* is best propagated by root cuttings. Because the species is so variable, it is best to ask the nursery for a description of the plant you are getting. Is it with lanceolate leaves or oval? Is it tall or short? Are the leaves wide or narrow? These questions should be asked if the plant is purchased by mail. We have ordered this plant from several sources and each time we received a slightly different variation on a theme. This plant is rangy in its growing habit, sending

out runners this way and that. It just spreads and spreads. Unfortunately, this habit makes it difficult to keep artemisia weed-free. It is a good idea to renew weedy beds every few years and to move plants to a different location. Crowding by weeds causes bottom foliage to turn brownish.

PICKING: Harvesting is done at the end of the season by cutting the plant right down to the ground. Two kinds of products are desirable. First, the white foliage is useful by itself either in arrangements or in wreaths. Second, one can opt for waiting until the inflorescence appears and then matures. These spikes of dull cream-colored flowers are also useful, albeit for a different effect. Definitely pick before heavy frosts or rains discolor the plant.

Artemisia
pontica
ROMAN WORMWOOD

COMMON NAME: Roman wormwood.
HISTORY: Originally from southeastern Europe, it has become naturalized in eastern North America. It is used to flavor vermouth and to decorate landscapes.
CULTIVATION: *A. pontica* is propagated primarily by root cuttings

early in the spring. Like *A. ludoviciana*, it has a rangy habit, growing here and there without any seemingly logical course. When used in garden landscapes, it should be contained because of its invasiveness. On rich soil, it produces a multitude of stems which give a mat-like appearance. On poor soil, it is sparse.

PICKING: Pick when full foliage is developed. This usually occurs at the end of the season but well before frosts come. Although it is a hardy plant, the foliage is apt to discolor with too much moisture and cold fall weather.

Artemisia schmidtiana
SILVER MOUND

COMMON NAME: Silver Mound.
HISTORY: Native to Japan, this plant is now cultivated throughout the world. Its primary use is in offsetting colorful annuals with its delicate feathery foliage and dense tufted appearance. The variety *nana* is a listed dwarf.
CULTIVATION: *A. schmidtiana* is propagated by root or stem cuttings early in the spring. Unlike *A. ludoviciana*, it does not spread, and requires several years to develop into a form that can be tapped for heavy propagation. It prefers to grow on elevated ground with low moisture con-

tent. With high moisture content or rich soil either the plant will rot in the early spring or its foliage will discolor at the end of the summer.
PICKING: It can be cut down to the ground either when the foliage is desired or when the inflorescence appears toward the end of the season. When tied in small bunches, it is much easier to separate after it is dry. The dried foliage and inflorescence are brittle, requiring especially delicate handling.

Artemisia vulgaris
MUGWORT

COMMON NAMES: mugwort, felon herb, St. John's herb.
HISTORY: Although most references sour at the mention of mugwort because of its weedy invasive habits, it can be quite useful as an everlasting. Originally from Europe and Asia, it is now quite prolific along roadsides in North America. Dried leaves of this plant were used in condiments, it was used to flavor beer, and, reducing the greasy taste of fatty poultry, it was used as a stuffing. Used in many pagan rituals to repel demons, it was also called Mother of Herbs. The common name is derived from the Old Saxon *muggia wort*, referring to its use in repelling insects. Chinese

use the leaves for treatment of rheumatism.
CULTIVATION: Propagated by seed, it quickly becomes a scourge of the garden. The best thing to do is to isolate the plant in a back border and to harvest the foliage before the plant flowers. It prefers medium quality soil but will survive in gravelly sand.
PICKING: Harvesting is best done before inflorescence develops. When dried, the leaves, brownish on top and silvery green on the bottom, give a nice texture and color to wreaths. If inflorescence is desired, the plant should be harvested to the ground before seed is formed, otherwise *caveat hortulanus*.

Asclepias tuberosa
BUTTERFLY WEED

COMMON NAMES: butterfly weed, pleurisy root, tuber-root, Indian paintbrush, chigger flower, swallow-wort.
HISTORY: The genus is named for Aesculapius, the ancient god of medicine. Until recently, this weed was listed in the U.S. Pharmacopoeia as a medicinal plant. It was utilized in the treatment of pleurisy and as a poultice on open sores. Indians boiled young shoots for food. A feature of the genus is a milky sap exuded by broken plant parts. This relative of common milkweed is but one of 200 species of this genus native to Africa and North America. *A. tu-*

Stachys byzantina surrounded by *Artemisia schmidtiana*. *Centaurea montana* in foreground.

berosa is found wild from New England to northern Mexico.

CULTIVATION: The plant is propagated by seed and by root division; however, once planted, it does not like to be disturbed. Sometimes, it will bloom from seed in the first year. It will grow on good or medium quality soil.

PICKING: *Asclepias* will dry well if the orange and red blossoms are picked when fully open but before they start to go by. Because they are fairly moist, they should be dried quickly. Unlike its relative the common milkweed, *A. syriaca*, this flower retains its color well.

Astilbe × arendsii
ASTILBE

COMMON NAMES: astilbe, spirea, false goatsbeard.

HISTORY: This is one of approximately 14 species of perennial herbs native to North America and eastern Asia. *Arendsii* is applied to one of several plants which are hybrids, resulting from crosses between *A. chinensis* var. *davidii* and several other species. Some *Astilbe* can be found in the wild. The cultivated varieties range in color from white to pinkish purple. The name of the genus comes from the Greek meaning opaque, not shining.

CULTIVATION: *Astilbe* prefers rich moist soil and light shade but will tolerate elevated acidity and some sun. It may be grown from seed or propagated from root cuttings early in the spring. Do not allow the plant to dry out.

PICKING: The flowers are panicled. They form a dense large spike that blooms from the bottom. That spike should be picked when approximately two-thirds developed. The flowers do not contain much moisture, usually drying without a problem.

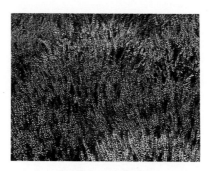

Calluna vulgaris
HEATHER

COMMON NAMES: heather, ling.

HISTORY: The genus name comes from the Greek meaning to sweep, referring to the use of its branches as brooms. There is only one species in the genus. *Calluna* is native to Europe and Asia Minor but is now cultivated in many parts of North America. In some parts of the northeastern U.S. it

has become acclimatized, performing well in sandy acidic soil on hills, rocky ledges and some peat bogs. Long used in European folk medicine, it has primarily an antibacterial effect.

Varieties grown for drying—available in colors from white to reddish—should be double-

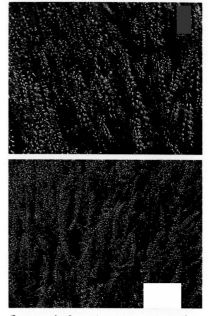

flowered for the greatest color effect.

CULTIVATION: Heather prefers acid soil and lots of air circulation to prevent mildew and fungus on the foliage. Most cultivated heathers are propagated by stem cuttings early in the spring and sometimes in late summer (if sufficient moisture—not standing water—is present in the rooting medium).

Calluna vulgaris creates a colorful tapestry—with minimal soil and fuss.

suggests, it could also refer to the brilliant colors and patterns that are found in Indian blankets.

CULTIVATION: These germinate from seed and are propagated by root division in the spring. Although perennial, they should not be cultivated in soil that is very wet, because the crowns may rot. They do, however, enjoy rich soil and produce abundant flowers all summer long.

PICKING: It is the flower pods, after the petals have lost their vigor, that should be picked. Pods retain some of the color from the flower, often a yellow or a red circular stripe. If picked shortly after flowering, the bud will stay strong and the conical shape will be useful in arrangements.

Goniolimon tataricum
GERMAN STATICE

COMMON NAME: German statice.
HISTORY: There are about 40 species in this genus. Most are native to the U.S.S.R. east to Mongolia, some to North Africa. This species is native from North Africa to the Caucasus and the U.S.S.R. The genus is closely allied to *Limonium* in form of styles and stig-

mas (see other descriptions under *Limonium*). The color of the flowers is light pink, drying to almost white.

CULTIVATION: Follow instructions under *Limonium* (the success with germination is a bit higher than with *Limonium*). There is still a problem with heaving and root breakage in the spring and fall. Another problem encountered is in the damage due to wind during the flowering time, when the spike is too heavy for the roots to support. The plant does set out side shoots, but there are not enough to count on these as the sole method of propagation. Survival in northern regions can be improved by as much as 90 percent by setting out plants on plastic mulch. The plant desires moisture, air circulation and sun in order to thrive.

PICKING: This is a finicky plant to grow for its flowers. Under normal circumstances, flowers should be picked when the spike is almost totally developed—they open a bit after picking. During dry periods, the flowers do not develop properly. Therefore, they should be treated as cut flowers—placed in warm water and allowed to develop. As soon as they are fully open, they should be hung to dry.

Gypsophila paniculata
BABY'S BREATH

COMMON NAME: baby's breath.
HISTORY: Native to an area from

Central Europe to Central Asia, specifically to Siberian regions and south, near Budapest, this is primarily the one out of some 125 species that is useful for drying. *G. elegans* is cultivated as a cut flower for the florist trade (not at

all useful as a flower for drying). Several varieties are listed, including large-flowering—propagated by cuttings—compact and double-flowered. The genus name describes its soil preferences; it prefers lime and calcareous soil and thrives in the sun.

CULTIVATION: Although this plant germinates well from seed, it grows slowly, blooming usually in the second year but sometimes in the third. Transplanting is chancy and, if done at all, should be accomplished early in the spring before the tops start developing. Late to come up—sometimes early in June—it should be marked with stakes in the fall for subsequent transplanting. Among the seeds, there are often a few of double-flowering varieties. The plant will flower for a period of time but will eventually get tired.

PICKING: *Gypsophila* should be picked when the flowers along the panicles are fully developed. It is also best to harvest around midday, when all the flowers that will open, open. Picking is essential to stretching the period of bloom.

Heuchera sanguinea in the foreground, painted daisies (*Chrysanthemum coccineum*) and iris in the background.

Heuchera sanguinea
CORAL BELLS

COMMON NAMES: coral bells, alumroot.

HISTORY: Named for Dr. H. Heucher of Wittenberg (1677-1747), professor of medicine, this genus is native to North America but especially the West. There are about 50 species, which thrive in open hilly and mountainous regions. They are hardy in rocky soil and are often grown in rock gardens.

CULTIVATION: This species has spikes of flowers with cultivars ranging in color from white to crimson. *Grandiflora* has larger flowers. The seed is like powder, very difficult to control in seeding. Seeding should be done sparingly and on top of moist soil. It is a good idea to trap some humidity

in the seed flat with a glass cover. Germination is good with fresh seed, but the seed may germinate idiosyncratically from one end of the flat to the other. It transplants well, but does not like soil with any standing water.

PICKING: *Heuchera* is a spike that blooms from the bottom. It should be picked before it opens fully. Its flowers dry well, shrinking a bit. The color gets slightly darker in drying, but the fragile, sparse, airy blooms are well worth drying.

Hydrangea paniculata
HYDRANGEA

COMMON NAMES: hydrangea, hortensia.

HISTORY: There are approximately 23 species in this genus of deciduous shrubs native to North and South America and eastern Asia. *H. paniculata* is native to China and Japan, with the *grandiflora* as the commonly cultivated form. It is known for the large, ten-inch-long clusters of white sterile flowers which turn color from pink to bronze when the nights begin to get cool. *H. macrophylla* produces flowers that are blue when the soil is acid and pink if the soil is alkaline.

CULTIVATION: This bush is known for the little care it needs to make it thrive. It prefers moist soil and will tolerate partial shade. The bush develops the most magnificent flowers in climates where humidity is plentiful. Even its genus name refers to its preference for moist environments, coming from the Greek meaning water vessel.

Some varieties bloom late and others early. On some species the flower bearing occurs on the new season's growth; on others, the growth is on buds set the previous year. The cultivars are propagated by soft stem cuttings, most successfully in the spring.

PICKING: The small flowers in the center of some clusters are fertile. These do not provide a desirable material for drying. The large flowers are sterile. If picked too soon they shrivel up, becoming useless. When the nights get cool, just before frost, the flowers change color and acquire a papery texture. That is the time to pick hydrangeas for drying. Generally, at this stage of development, there is little moisture in the flower, so it dries quickly. But drying it over a stove or with fans will not necessarily result in a more attractive flower. It is the stage of development that determines one's success. Our indicator is the pinkish color of the clusters on the outside of the bush. At that stage, even the white clusters toward the center of the bush have less moisture. They will keep the color well. For an earth-tone effect, pick some bronze hydrangeas after frost. The form is the same, and quite attractive. The color is cream or golden brown, fitting well with wreaths made of goldenrod and tansy.

Hyssopus officinalis
HYSSOP

COMMON NAME: hyssop.

HISTORY: There are several varieties of hyssop, one of the earliest

Hydrangea paniculata grandiflora

plants to be recorded in herbals. It is native to Southern Europe but has been cultivated in herb gardens as a remedy for various discomforts (mentioned by Paulus Aeginita in the seventh century), as an essential plant in the Elizabethan knot gardens and mentioned in French literature as a component in manufacturing eau de cologne. There is also a reference to *azob* (source of its botanical name) as a holy herb of ancient Hebrews; however, their description does not satisfactorily fit any of the species of hyssop presently known. Thus, it is possible that various ancient plants were clumped into an identity of what is now known as hyssop. The plant is cultivated in Europe, Russia and India for teas and medicines. The various varieties of *H. officinalis* are primarily differentiated by the color of the flowers—white, rose, red and light purple.

CULTIVATION: According to various sources, hyssop does well in dry sweet soil. We have found that it also thrives in rich soil as long as it is not fertilized after the end of July—a rule that applies to all perennials. The rich soil is responsible for larger and more vibrant colors as well as larger plants. Propagation is well accomplished by seed or by stem cuttings. Seeds are always plentiful at the end of the season and can be used as the chief method of propagation. If the seeds are started early enough in winter or spring, blooms can be expected in August of the first year; otherwise, they will come too late for sufficient production. Hyssop is a beautiful plant and should be considered as a decorative or an evergreen hedge plant in every garden. In four to five years it gets woody and may need to be trimmed back.

PICKING: Flowers can be picked as they are developing and when they are open approximately two-thirds of the way up the spike. The color is most vibrant when the flowers are dried quickly; however, hyssop has a low moisture content and will dry readily anyway. In using hyssop as a design element, one will enjoy not only a beautiful flower but also a wonderful sweet, minty aroma.

Lavandula angustifolia
LAVENDER

COMMON NAME: English lavender.

HISTORY: There are about 20 species of lavender originally native to an area from the Mediterranean to Somalia. Its sweet aroma has been known for centuries and is thought to have been mentioned by Virgil under the name *cafia*. Gerard suggests that all should share the virtues of the strong fragrance of lavender: "About them let fresh lavender and the store of wild Time with strong Savorie to floure." Used in medicine and for decoration, lavender is certainly a desirable plant. At present, *L. angustifolia* and *L. stoechas* (a biennial variety from Stoechades, the Iles de Hyères),

known as Cassidony, are used in perfumes. As a highly valued plant, it gave rise to the saying "Do it up in lavender," to indicate special care and attention.

Many writers suggest that the genus name is Latin in origin, referring to the verb *lavito, lavitare*, meaning to wash. Middle Latin, however, doesn't seem to indicate the derivation of the word and contemporary students of etymology speculate that since medieval *lavandula* is also spelled *livendula*, it is possible that the word comes from the classical Latin *liveo, livere*, meaning bluish.

CULTIVATION: *L. angustifolia* is variably hardy in northern regions. It is a delicate plant but one that will survive if certain precautions are taken. Lavender grows well on raised beds; it does not like standing water or wet roots. In fact, it prefers soil that is rich but dry. Also, protecting it from early thaw, late erratic freezes and dehydrating winds will increase its chances of survival. One should not mulch the upper part of the plant with leaves or other dense material; that may

cause mildew and fungus which eventually kill the plant.

Lavender can be propagated by seed or by stem cuttings in the spring. The germination rate is generally poor and spotty; the seeds germinate over a long period of time. It is best to plant the seeds on top of the soil and allow exposure to light—the seeds are light-sensitive—and then cover the tray with a piece of glass or plastic. The best germination occurs at temperatures warmer than ambient room temperature.

PICKING: As a dry flower lavender has a desirable aroma, but the color, in comparison with *Salvia farinacea*, is quite subdued. Therefore, it is used less for design than for providing a wreath or an arrangement with a dimension of fragrance. Drying lavender is not complex. It should be picked before the bottom flowers have matured, because they easily fall off. The bunches should not be large, for the flowers tangle up and are delicate and difficult to separate.

Leontopodium alpinum
EDELWEISS

COMMON NAME: edelweiss.

HISTORY: The genus *Leontopodium* is complex in that the names of a great number of species are used interchangeably by various authors. In some older sources it is classified with *Gnaphalium*. The true genus name is derived from the Greek *leon*, lion, and *pous*, foot, in reference to the shape of

the flower head. The flower is associated with many sentimental and mysterious stories from the Alps, where it grows under cliffs. The flower is quite inconspicuous, if marginally interesting. The plant is not prolific and, in some areas, variably hardy.

CULTIVATION: *Leontopodium* can be propagated by its scarce seeds or by root division. The plant, if started from seed early in the season, will produce blooms the first year. It prefers sweet sandy soil but will survive in loose loam.

PICKING: Pick the flower heads when they are young, but with flowers already open. If the plant is in full sun, it will have a greenish-gray appearance. If it is grown in partial shade, it will be light gray.

Liatris pycnostachya
LIATRIS

COMMON NAMES: liatris, blazing-star, button-snakeroot, gay-feather, devilsbit, colic-root, rattlesnake master.

HISTORY: Native to North America, this genus contains 40 species. The derivation of the genus name is unknown. The species name means thick-spiked. This species is quite attractive because it has wide and full spikes of flowers. They come in white and

reddish purple. Unlike most spike flowers, which bloom from the bottom up, *Liatris* blooms from the top down. Bees and butterflies are attracted to the flowers of a plant that stands out in the garden because of its unusual color and shape. Useful for its antibacterial properties, *Liatris* was used in New England as a treatment for venereal disease; also, the roots and leaves were powdered and used to repel insects.

CULTIVATION: Known for its resilience, the plant will survive under a variety of soil and light conditions; drought and heat will not bother it. For producing the most blooms, however, it prefers rich moist soil (but not standing water early in the spring) and sunlight. There are several ways to propagate: seeds that germinate readily, root division and offset plants. It blooms in the second year from seed.

PICKING: Since *Liatris* blooms from the top down, it should be picked before the top goes by. If picked too late, the color will turn darker and the seeds will fall out. If picked a bit early, the bottom flowers on the spike will not open as much as they could. Since it is a relative of *Eupatorium* (Joe-Pye weed), the bracts, left after the seeds fall out, will have a similar star-like iridescent appearance. But the spike without its flowers has little to recommend it for decoration.

Limonium latifolium
SEA LAVENDER

COMMON NAMES: sea lavender, marsh rosemary.

HISTORY: This plant, native to Rumania, Bulgaria and the southern U.S.S.R., resembles *L. caro-*

linianum (native to the seacoast of North America) in its form. However, this species will grow on sweet soil and is primarily the one found cultivated. The most obvious difference between the two is in the appearance of the stalks and the spacing of the flowers. The genus name comes from the Greek *leimon*, grassy plain.

CULTIVATION: This is a difficult plant to start from seed because the germination rate is so poor and the rate of development is variable. The best way to germinate is to place seed on top of the soil, seal in the humidity by covering the tray and increase the temperature of the heat mat to 75° F. Be careful to allow some air to circulate during the day, because the germinating plants easily damp off. Another way to propagate it is from root cuttings, once the plant is three to four years old. Started from seed, the plant flowers in two to three years.

Its hardiness is variable but has less to do with cold than dehydration and breakage of the roots due to heaving. Its lavender corollas and airy spikes make it a worthwhile plant in the garden.

PICKING: For best color retention, *Limonium* should be picked during the height of the day, when all the flowers that will open, open. This spike should be picked when it is approximately four-fifths de-

veloped, possibly even after the lower flowers have gone by. The open calyx that is left is still attractive and stays fast on the stem.

Lunaria annua
MONEY PLANT

COMMON NAMES: money plant, honesty, moonwort, satin flower, bolbonac, silver-dollar, honest pocketbook, money-in-both pockets, moon-penny, moon-dollar.

HISTORY: Actually a biennial species, this plant has been known to flower in its first year when started from seed. There are two listed species in this family relative of cabbages and mustards. *L. annua* is native to Southern Europe but has become naturalized in Europe and North America. It derives its genus name from the shape of the fruiting stems which are left after the seeds drop. Some botanical writers suggest that the plant has been in cultivation from the late sixteenth century. But others suggest that the *Lunaria* referred to by old writers was actually a different plant—a fern called moonwort, probably the one credited with magical properties and noted by Chaucer. The plant was also said to be good for falling sickness (epilepsy) and lunacy.

CULTIVATION: As with most Cruciferae, *Lunaria* is subject to club-

root, a fungal soil-borne disease. It should not be planted in the same space or in rotation with other members of its family. From seed, it germinates readily. However, because it uses up soil nutrition and grows rapidly, it should not be started in the greenhouse too early. A bit of stress may cause it to bloom in the first year. The soil should have sufficient lime; otherwise, the plant may rot at ground level. Best grown on raised beds, *Lunaria* needs room for air to circulate in order to prevent mold from forming on pods, making them useless as decoration.

PICKING: The best time to pick is after frost. At that time, the pods dry up and the seed is scattered,

leaving the thin membrane that is useful as an everlasting. However, if the season is moist, picking earlier, but well after seed is mature, may be the only alternative. But then the job of slipping the outer shells becomes tedious and time-consuming.

Malva
moschata
MALLOW

COMMON NAMES: mallow, musk mallow.

HISTORY: There are about 30 species in this genus of annual, bien-

nial and perennial herbs. Most are native to North Africa and Europe, but *M. moschata* has become naturalized in the eastern U.S. Most flowers are pink but some cultivars are white. Its genus name comes from the Greek *malache*, referring to the soft mucilaginous property of its leaves. The species name refers to the musky smell of the roots. In the sixteenth century, a close relative of this plant, *M. sylvestris*, was given the name *omnimorbia*, meaning a cure-all. The leaves were cooked as a vegetable and the seeds and their capsules were eaten in salads. Marsh mallow mucilage was used to flavor marshmallows.

CULTIVATION: This plant is easy to propagate from seed, but resists transplanting because of its deep taproot. Early in the spring, when the plant is still young, transplanting may be accomplished only if the prepared bed is well watered and the root is not allowed to dry out.

PICKING: Pods are picked either when they are green, eventually becoming creamy, or when they have produced seed, when they are papery dry. Use them in arrangements or wreaths.

Mentha spicata
SPEARMINT

COMMON NAME: spearmint.
HISTORY: Although there are over 600 named species in the genus of *Mentha*, many taxonomists believe that there are many variants of approximately 25 different species. *M. spicata*, also known as *M. viridis*, has been in cultivation for centuries. It is speculated that it was introduced to Northern Europe by the Romans. It was used for medicine and for cooking. The genus name is for the nymph Mentha, daughter of the river Cocytus. Because Pluto loved

her, Proserpine changed her into an herb. In France, spearmint is dedicated to the Virgin Mary under the name of Our Lady's mint (*menthe de Notre Dame*). Throughout Europe, it was used as a means for repaying debts and was even mentioned in the Bible as serving the same purpose.

CULTIVATION: Mints prefer moist and rich soil. Some do well in shade, but given the essential nutrients, they will do well in the sun. Most are propagated by seed; however, certain unusual varieties are propagated by root or stem cuttings, rooting readily in moist sand or water.

PICKING: The flowers are useful because they hold color well and give off a wonderful aroma. When the spikes are two-thirds developed, they should be picked. There are other plants in this genus useful for drying: *M.* × *piperita*, *M.* × *piperita* var. *citrata* (bergamot mint) and *M. rotundifolia* (apple mint).

Monarda fistulosa
BEE BALM

COMMON NAMES: bee balm, horsemint, wild bergamot, Oswego Tea.
HISTORY: In this genus, there are about 12 species of herbs that are native to North America and Mexico. Many species have become naturalized in South America. The common name bergamot comes from the resemblance in fragrance to the bergamot mint. The common name Oswego Tea carries a bit of American history. The plant was used medicinally by American Indians who lived near the Oswego River (they called it O-gee-chee). The famous Boston Tea Party of 1773 marked an era when some American colonists switched from the imported tea to Oswego Tea. The genus name is commemorative of Dr. Nicolas Bautista de Monardes (1493–1588) of Seville, an eminent Spanish physician, botanist and writer. The closely related species *M. didyma* has a red blossom. *M. fistulosa* flowers are light pink to purple. *Didyma* means paired and refers to the two stamens that protrude with the single pistil from the upper lip.
CULTIVATION: Plants start readily from seed as well as from root cuttings and division in the spring. The plant's natural habitat

Monarda fistulosa

is marshy areas. Rich soil and partial shade are preferred. Full sun produces larger clumps. Lots of air circulation reduces the potential for powdery mildew on leaves (an endemic feature of the plant). *M. didyma* is more likely than *M. fistulosa* to have a second tier of flowers on top of the bloom. If plants are cut back early after bloom, they will bloom again; however, if they produce pods, a second bloom is unlikely.

PICKING: Flowers should be picked when developed but young. Watch for the number of flowers developed from the edge to the center. If the flowers are old, the petals will fall off even more readily; they are delicate flowers. Pods can be picked after the bloom is over. Of course, the pods do not have the color range of the flowers.

Nepeta mussinii
CATMINT

COMMON NAME: catmint.
HISTORY: There are about 250 species of herbs belonging to this genus. Many are native to Europe, Asia and North Africa. Some are native to mountains of tropical Africa. Many plants of this genus are raised for medicinal reasons, others for teas, still others

for ground covers. This plant, along with its close relative *N. cataria*, is known for its effect on cats: they love eating it, rolling in it and certainly damaging it. Medicinally, *Nepeta* was used to treat infantile colic and diarrhea, headaches, stomachaches and flatulence. Women used it in baths. *N. mussinii* has by far a more desirable aroma and is delightful in tea. Its blue flowers dry beautifully, provided the cats do not climb the walls and ceiling to get at them. The genus name comes from Nepet, a town in Tuscany. The species name is for the Russian count Apollos Apollosovitch Mussin-Pushkin, who found it on an expedition to the Caucasus at the turn of the nineteenth century.

CULTIVATION: A plant that is easily started from seed or root division, it blooms readily in its first year. It is a hardy perennial except when allowed to go to seed and then severely cut back. Sweet rich soil with plenty of moisture will produce most attractive plants. A problem in cultivation is the feline population. They sometimes dig it up. The best remedy for that is to plant more than they can possibly consume.

PICKING: The four-inch spikes of blue flowers should be picked when they are approximately four-fifths developed. They dry quickly as long as bunches are not too large.

Origanum vulgare
OREGANO

COMMON NAME: oregano.
HISTORY: There are actually more than 15 species in this genus, including another useful herb for drying, *Origanum majorana* (marjoram), an annual. Both are indig-

enous to North Africa and southwestern Asia. The genus name comes from the Greek and means mountain joy. The species name *majorana* is of unknown derivation; *vulgare* means common. Marjoram has a long and elaborate history. The legend is that Greeks planted it on the graves of ancestors to bestow upon them restful sleep. Newlyweds wore crowns of marjoram because the scent was said to have emanated from the touch of Venus. It was used in perfumery, in cooking and as a strewing herb in monasteries—to fill the damp and gloomy chambers with a fresh sweet scent.

CULTIVATION: A great deal of confusion exists in the classification and assigning of common names to *Origanum* species. Marjoram is an annual. *Origanum vulgare* is a hardy perennial growing to three feet in good moist soil. Marjoram flowers are white, purplish or pink enclosed in a greenish calyx. But since the species is variable, it may resemble that of common or wild oregano. One thing is certain: marjoram will not survive northern winters, whereas oregano will. The fragrance of marjoram is sweet; that of common oregano is minty. Both like rich soil, but marjoram has a tendency to be susceptible to root rot and damping-off in extremely moist soils. Also, when started from seed, seedlings are delicate. They should have plenty of air circulation and porous, almost sandy soil.

PICKING: Flowers of both marjoram and oregano should be picked when they are in full bloom— usually a week or two after the commencement of flowering. The flowers are small and inconspicuous, but the shading and tonality are there, giving fragrance and delicate shading to wreaths.

*Papaver
orientale*
ORIENTAL POPPY

COMMON NAME: Oriental poppy.
HISTORY: More than 50 species exist in this genus of annual and perennial herbs. Most of them are native to the Old World. The genus name is derived from the Latin *pap*, in reference to the thick milky substance exuded by the stem or pods; infants were given seeds and pap in food to make them sleep. Another theory as to the origin of its name suggests that it comes from the sounds made when the seed is chewed. Its close relative *P. somniferum* is known as the opium poppy, whose cultivation is illegal in the United States. *P. orientale* is native to southwestern Asia and is a showy plant that flowers in the spring. It was first found in Armenia by Tournefort, a French botanist. Its seeds were sent to growers in England and Holland in the early eighteenth century.

CULTIVATION: After they stop flowering, the plants become shaggy and unattractive. But then the pod is left. Propagation is by seed, which is scattered where it is to grow, or by root division in the spring. Although some sources suggest that seedlings do not transplant well, the feat can be accomplished if the seeds are started early in the spring and grown at cool temperatures. They usually bloom in the second year. Flowers are short-lived and the stems usually droop when battered by brisk spring winds. Moist

soil, but no standing water, with good nutrients, will produce the largest flowers and pods.
PICKING: Pods should be picked when they have reached maturity, but before they turn brown. If left out too long, they may start to mildew and discolor. Pods keep their shape and are attractive in arrangements.

*Physalis
alkekengi*
CHINESE LANTERN

COMMON NAMES: Chinese lantern, alkekengi, Japanese lantern, winter cherry, strawberry tomato, bladder cherry.
HISTORY: Of the 80 species in this genus, some are known for culinary, some for medicinal and

some for decorative uses. In Europe, to which it is native, this plant was cultivated as early as the first century A.D. The genus name comes from the Greek meaning bladder and the species name is the same as that used by Dioscorides, although it originally came from Arabic and is of obscure origin. For culinary purposes, *Physalis* was used in jams and preserves. Medicinally, it was

used as a diuretic, but later its value was discredited. It was also used in garlands in Europe. Victorian ladies soaked *Physalis* pods to macerate the calyx and expose the red berry. In the United States it was also raised commercially for decoration.
CULTIVATION: Propagated as easily from seed as by root division, *Physalis* is a winter-hardy plant. Usually it blooms from seed in its second year. To start it from seed, give it the same conditions as you

OVERLEAF *Pycnanthemum incanum*

tims. In the Middle Ages, similar practices were followed, but with criminals rather than victims. In Italy, it was used to adorn dead infants. In ancient Greece, myrtle, ivy and narcissus were used for burial crowns on the heads of a reference in an old ballad: "A garlande of Pervenke set on his heved"), or because of the way it creeps over other plants. The genus name *Vinca* is from the Latin *vincula*, a band. Chaucer referred to the glossy foliage of *Vinca* as "fresh Pervinke rich of hew." The plant is a hardy evergreen perennial with purple or white flowers and glossy rich green foliage appearing early in the spring. The flowers do not dry except by pressing, and the leaves for best use in design are those where tissues have become tough with fall frosts. If young spring leaves are picked, they will not dry without wrinkling.

CULTIVATION: Commercially, the plant is propagated by root division or by cuttings. It prefers shady moist soil and will do well without much care.

PICKING: This plant is useful for its foliage. The rich green is a rare commodity among everlastings. The color is fast for about six months and then it begins to fade to light olive and finally to cream. Picking can be done just before a wreath is made, or the leaves can be woven when they are dry. The advantage of working with the fresh material is that it is not brittle and the leaves do not dry absolutely flat; this contributes to a natural appearance. If it is to be dried before use, myrtle can be laid out on a screen or hung in bunches.

At Wolf's Neck Farm in Freeport, Maine, everlastings are used for landscaping, for cutting, and for drying.

Gardener's Guide for Perennial Everlastings

PAGE NUMBER	GENUS	SPECIES	COMMON NAME	HEIGHT	PLANTING DISTANCE	PART USED
72	Achillea	filipendulina	golden yarrow	4'	2'	flower
72–73	Achillea	millefolium	yarrow	3'	2'	flower
73	Achillea	millefolium	rose yarrow	3'	2'	flower
73–74	Achillea	ptarmica	the pearl	2'	18"	flower
74	Achillea	tomentosa	woolly yarrow	18"	12"	flower
74	Alchemilla	vulgaris	lady's mantle	18"	12"	flower
74–76	Allium	ampeloprasum	leek	3'	6"	flower
74–76	Allium	cepa	onion	3'	6"	flower
74–76	Allium	schoenoprasum	chive	18"	6"	flower
74–76	Allium	tuberosum	garlic chive	18"	6"	flower
76–77	Anaphalis	margaritacea	pearly everlasting	18"	12"	flower
77	Aquilegia	×hybrida	columbine	2"	18"	pod
77–80	Armeria	maritima	armeria	12"	6"	flower
80–81	Artemisia	absinthium	wormwood, common	6'	3'	foliage
81	Artemisia	ludoviciana	artemisia, Silver King	2'	12"	plant
81	Artemisia	ludoviciana	artemisia, Silver Queen	2'	12"	foliage
81–82	Artemisia	pontica	wormwood, Roman	12"	12"	foliage
82	Artemisia	schmidtiana	Silver Mound	12"	18"	foliage
80	Artemisia	spicata	Artemisia genipi	6"	6"	flower
82	Artemisia	vulgaris	mugwort	6'	3'	foliage
82–84	Asclepias	tuberosa	butterfly weed	3'	12"	flower
84	Astilbe	×arendsii	astilbe	4'	2'	flower
84	Calluna	vulgaris	heather	2'	2'	flower
86	Carlina	acaulis	Carline thistle	6"	12"	flower
86–87	Catananche	caerulea	catananche	2'	12"	pod
87	Celastrus	scandens	bittersweet	30'	5'	fruit
87	Centaurea	macrocephala	globe centaurea	3'	18"	flower and bud
87–88	Chrysanthemum	parthenium	matricaria	3'	18"	flower
87–88	Chrysanthemum	parthenium	golden feverfew	18"	18"	flower
88	Cimicifuga	racemosa	black cohosh	6'	3'	flower and pod
88–89	Cirsium	japonicum	thistle	3'	18"	flower
89	Coreopsis	lanceolata	coreopsis	3'	3'	pod
89–90	Cortaderia	selloana	pampas grass	6'	2'	flower
90	Delphinium	×cultorum	delphinium	5'	3'	flower
90–91	Dipsacus	fullonum	teasel	6'	2'	pod
91	Echinops	ritro	globe thistle	4'	2'	flower
91	Eryngium	planum	sea holly	18"	18"	flower
91–92	Gaillardia	×grandiflora	gaillardia	2'	18"	pod
92	Goniolimon	tataricum	German statice	18"	12"	flower
92	Gypsophila	paniculata	baby's breath	3'	3'	flower
94	Heuchera	sanguinea	coral bells	2'	18"	flower
94	Hydrangea	paniculata	hydrangea	20'	20'	flower
94–96	Hyssopus	officinale	hyssop	2'	2'	flower
96–97	Lavandula	angustifolia	lavender	18"	18"	flower
97	Leontopodium	alpinum	edelweiss	12"	6"	flower
97	Liatris	pycnostachya	blazing-star	4'	2'	flower
97–99	Limonium	latifolium	sea lavender	2'	12"	flower
99	Lunaria	annua	honesty	2'	18"	pod
99–100	Malva	moschata	mallow	5'	3'	pod
100	Mentha	spicata	spearmint	3'	3'	flower
100–102	Monarda	fistulosa	bee balm	5'	2'	flower and pod
102	Nepeta	mussinii	catmint	12"	18"	flower
102	Origanum	vulgare	oregano	3'	3'	flower
103	Papaver	orientale	Oriental poppy	3'	2'	pod
103	Physalis	alkekengi	Chinese lantern	4'	2'	pod
106	Physostegia	virginiana	obedient plant	2'	2'	pod
106	Poterium	sanguisorba	burnet	18"	18"	flower
106–107	Pycnanthemum	incanum	mountain mint	2'	2'	flower
107	Rosa	spp.	rose	var.	var.	flower and pod
107–108	Rudbeckia	hirta	gloriosa daisy	18"	12"	pod

PAGE NUMBER	GENUS	SPECIES	COMMON NAME	HEIGHT	PLANTING DISTANCE	PART USED
108	Ruta	graveolens	rue	2′	18″	flower and pod
108–109	Salvia	officinalis	sage	2′	18″	flower and pod
109	Salvia	×superba	salvia	18″	12″	flower
110	Sedum	spectabile	sedum	18″	12″	flower
110	Stachys	byzantina	lamb's ears	2′	18″	flower and foliage
89–90	Stipa	avenacea	black oat-grass	2′	12″	flower
89–90	Stipa	pennata	European feather grass	2′	12″	flower
110–111	Tanacetum	vulgare	tansy	5′	2′	flower
111–112	Vinca	major	myrtle	6″	12″	foliage

Dipsacus fullonum pod

5

Picking in the Wild

Some of our most
pleasurable summer days
are spent collecting flowers
and pods in the wild. During the
summer, when a change of scenery
is in order, everyone looks forward
to getting away from the demands of the
garden—the constant regime of maintenance
and harvesting. But the wilds of which we speak
are not necessarily miles away. The wilds may be as
near as a few feet from the cultivated garden—a winding
country road, a swampy marshland replete with buzzing
insects and even such unlikely places as abandoned railroad
beds or parking lots. On the other hand, the wilds may be
truly magical places—a sea marsh with herons flying

overhead or deer scampering about; a mountaintop with a dark blue sky and clouds that hug the rolling hills.

In the wild, we are a part of nature. We are a part of a tradition that called on people to discover, enjoy and partake of their environment. Picking in the wild is also a different kind of an investment. Where but in the wild can we, on a whim, try out a new plant to see whether it will dry? In the garden, it takes months from sowing to harvest. When we pick in the wild, we can evaluate the usefulness of a plant in a few days.

For the apartment dweller, the wild plants may become an even more valuable resource. You need not spend any time in the garden to have everlasting arrangements or wreaths. Plants that can be picked in the wild offer subtle color and contrasting shapes. Often the subdued effects that are created with collected plants are necessary to complete designs using the more obvious colors and shapes of cultivars. In fact, even if you do have a garden, collecting wild plants should be an important consideration because the sheer volume of material that is available in the wild is difficult to obtain from the garden without a great deal of tedious work. No matter how much material we raise, no matter how many varieties we produce, the non-cultivated plants that we pick are integral to dry flower design.

Often people refer to collecting plants in the wild as picking weeds. But the word "weed" is pejorative, if not inappropriate. The term implies that the plant is not desirable; that it has no innate merit; that it hinders. However, not all wild plants are weeds and not all weeds are wild plants—as

anyone who has tried to grow rapidly spreading mints would agree. Perhaps those of us who are preoccupied with weeds should reflect on a definition by Ralph Waldo Emerson, who in 1878 said that a weed is "a plant whose virtues have not yet been discovered." For those who are interested in nature, wildflowers or everlastings, James Russell Lowell's judgment is even more appropriate: "A weed is no more than a flower in disguise."

Plants in the wild are a tangible resource in that they contribute to the beauty of our environment. What is more, they are also functional. They provide nutrition for birds and other animals. They stem erosion and loss of soil disturbed by man or nature. They sustain and shelter insects. They indicate soil quality and add to it by their annual decay. They are a distinct aspect of our ecology that should be nourished and protected.

Readers of this chapter will notice that many flowers, herbs and shrubs are alien to the soils of the United States. Some have come as stowaways among the seeds that were brought by European colonists. Some have escaped cultivation. Others have always been here to be used by Native Americans for food, flavoring, medicine or dye.

Picking in the wild should be done thoughtfully. It requires a sensitivity toward your environment, a knowledge of plants and an awareness of their relationship to man. Collecting and harvesting should be done carefully.

There are some simple rules to follow when picking in the wild. First, keep in mind that the land and its plant life belong to someone. Try to find the owner and ask whether there are

any objections to your picking. Chances are that the objections will be minimal, but it could also be that the owner will prefer that even some common weeds, such as goldenrod, be left standing. One inquiry may create a friend; an omission may cause hard feelings.

Second, some species of plants are rare and others are abundant. Before venturing out, familiarize yourself with the protected plants and be sure to leave them undisturbed. Injury to a rare specimen may be injury to the species. Common or prolific plants should also command respect. Nothing in our environment is infinite, and abuse of even plentiful species may result in a disaster. Pick conservatively.

Most plants propagate either sexually or by division. If a plant is damaged, it will not send out runners. If a field is overpicked, it may not yield future generations—all the seeds will have been harvested. Although it is difficult to leave some plants in a good stand, it is important to do so, because seeds contribute genetic variability and thereby allow different species to adapt to stressful climatic changes. Always leave a good portion of plants undisturbed.

Third, a plant should be harvested with the aid of a sharp knife, scissors or shears. A sharp instrument ensures a smooth cut and discourages the natural instinct to pull on a plant, dislodging roots and breaking tubers. Pulling not only may destroy that particular plant but may also affect how plentiful a species will be in the future. Trampling of plants or lack of care will not leave any plants to be harvested in future seasons.

With some encouragement

and some pointers, we suggest that you try picking the following plants in the wild. By no means is this a definitive list (some wild plants, e.g. *Achillea* and *Anaphalis*, are listed in Chapter 4), but it will start you on your way. You will undoubtedly discover many more species, for gathering in the wild will open up a whole new area of interest in the discovery of plant life.

Antennaria neglecta
PUSSY-TOES

COMMON NAMES: pussy-toes, cat's foot, life everlasting, cud-weed, ladies' tobacco.

HISTORY: *Antennaria* resembles a miniature *Gnaphalium* (it was first classified under *Gnaphalium*). The genus is difficult to classify into species because there is a fair amount of plasticity, or variation. There are about 75 species of these common weedy plants that are adapted to poor, dry soil. The genus is indigenous to North America, Northern Europe and Northern Asia. Certain members of the genus are sometimes found cultivated in rock gardens, where they are often grown for the use of flowers as everlastings. *A. dioica* was used by Indians to treat mouth ulcers. The genus name comes from the Latin meaning

antenna-like. The species name means that it is a neglected plant. A feature of this genus is parthenogenesis—reproduction without fertilization.

PERIOD OF BLOOM: April to June.
PICKING: Picking such small and low-growing plants is quite tedious, and the volume is low. They should be picked before the buds open to reveal the center of the flower. Closely related to *Gnaphalium*, *Anaphalis* and certain species of *Helichrysum*, they dry in a similar manner—opening up after picking.

Artemisia stelleriana
DUSTY MILLER

COMMON NAMES: dusty miller, beach wormwood.

HISTORY: Native to northeastern Asia and the coast of Sweden, it is now cultivated in seacoast gardens. See *Artemisia* in Chapter 4.

PERIOD OF BLOOM: July to August.

PICKING: Spikes of inflorescence are few. Pick them before the flowers have all gone by.

Asclepias syriaca
MILKWEED

COMMON NAMES: common milk-weed, silkweed, wild cotton.

HISTORY: See *Asclepias* in Chapter 4.

PERIOD OF BLOOM: June to August.

PICKING: Pick pods when they are just opening up or after they have been bleached by the fall sun.

Campanula rapunculoides
CAMPANULA

COMMON NAMES: campanula, rover bellflower, creeping bell-flower.

HISTORY: Found along roadsides and fields of North America, this

A front lawn, a seacoast, or a forgotten city lot can be a welcome source of materials for drying. At left is *Antennaria*. At top right is *Artemisia stelleriana*. At bottom right are *Cirsium* and *Lepidium* pods.

A sea marsh, *left*, and a sweet water marsh, *right*, have many plants for drying.

Rarely, however, is it found in the same area as *Anaphalis*, which prefers higher altitudes and cooler temperatures.

PERIOD OF BLOOM: August to September.

PICKING: As with *Helichrysum* and *Anaphalis*, *Gnaphalium* should be picked while it is still budded, in order to retain the maximum color intensity. If picked too late, the center will puff out and only the outside bracts will remain. The sweet fragrance makes this plant highly desirable, not only for wreaths but also for arrangements and potpourri.

Hieracium aurantiacum
and
H. villosum
HAWKWEED

COMMON NAMES: orange hawkweed, yellow hawkweed, devil's paintbrush, king-devil, tawny hawkweed, golden mouse-ear hawkweed, grim-the-collier, red daisy, missionary weed.

HISTORY: This genus contains between 700 and 1,000 species. Most are native to the Northern Hemisphere, but some are found in southern India, Africa and South America. Most are troublesome weeds, but some are cultivated in rock gardens because they are resistant to drought. Un-

fortunately, they are also persistent, dividing by seed and stolons. The genus name comes from the Greek *hierax*, hawk or falcon. *Aurantiacum* means orange; *villosum* means hairy (this species is yellow).

PERIOD OF BLOOM: June to September.

PICKING: Unlike *Emilia javanica*, which holds its color and if picked at the right time will not feather out, hawkweed is difficult to pick. Some heads, if picked in the early stages of maturity, will retain their color. But the heads have many flowers at different stages of development, so it is difficult to get it just right. In a wildflower wreath, this flower may still be attractive.

Iris versicolor
IRIS

COMMON NAMES: iris, blue flag, poison flag, water flag, snake liver, flag lily, liver lily, flower-de-luce.

HISTORY: This plant is found wild in eastern North America. However, there are many other species that produce beautiful pods for decoration. *Iris* thrives in moist areas and in marshes. In this genus there are about 200 species that, when cultivated, are raised primarily as ornamentals. Some Old World species are used in the production of powdered orris and in perfumery. *I. versicolor* has been used by Indians to treat

gastric disturbances, but as some of the common names suggest, it is not a plant to use in cooking or for medicine. Used as a dye plant to produce browns and blacks, *Iris* has been known to and cultivated by man through the ages. In different cultures, the plant has been consecrated to the devil and to Jove. *Fleur-de-lis* (*Iris* × *germanica*) was sacred to the Virgin. The French common name *fleur-de-lis* is thought by some to be a corruption of *fleur-de-Luce* and *fleur-de-Louis*, referring to King Louis VII of France, who used it on his heraldic emblem when he set out on the Second Crusade. Others attributed this common name to the corruption of *délices*, flower of delights.

PERIOD OF BLOOM: June to July.

PICKING: The pod is picked as it is shedding its seeds.

Juncus canadensis
RUSH

COMMON NAME: Canada rush.

HISTORY: There are approximately 240 species in this genus.

J. canadensis, which is native to North America, is found in wet places, and its relatives are prolific in both freshwater and saltwater marshes. The genus name comes from the Latin *jungo*, to bind, in reference to their use as material for binding or tying. Rushes differ from grasses and sedges in the size of the family, having fewer members, and in readily identifiable morphology—they have flowers that resemble a lily, with three petals and three sepals, and their fruit stays on the plant for most of the season.

PERIOD OF BLOOM: Middle to late summer.

PICKING: Pick the pod shortly after bloom to retain some green color.

Lechea racemulosa
PIN WEED

COMMON NAME: pin weed.

HISTORY: Growing on rocky or sandy soil, this plant may be found east of the Mississippi. The family Cistaceae (rock roses) contains several cultivated genera, including *Cistus* and *Helianthemum*. The genus name is commemorative of G. Leche, a Swedish bot-

anist who died in 1764. Pin weeds are native to North America.

PERIOD OF BLOOM: July to August.

PICKING: Pick when the plant has fully flowered but before the bottom flowers are about to fall off. The plant is dry to begin with and is thus not difficult to dry. The flowers do not continue to develop.

Lepidium campestre and spp.
PEPPER GRASS

COMMON NAMES: pepper grass, yellow seed, Mithridate mustard, glen pepper, poor-man's pepper, glen weed, crowd weed, false flax, field cress, cow cress, bastard cress.

HISTORY: This genus contains more than 100 species of annual and perennial herbs. They are found mostly in temperate regions but are widespread. *L. campestre* is naturalized in the United States, having come from Europe. Inhabiting waste places and disturbed soils, this species thrives where little if any nutrition exists. Actually, many members of the Cruciferae family produce interesting and graceful pods. These pods may be elongate or scale-like and may be found in the wild—look for *Alliaria officinalis* (garlic mustard), *Capsella bursa-pastoris* (shepherd's purse) or *Thlaspi arvense* (field pennycress); they may be found in the backyard—watch cabbage, Chinese cabbage or radishes go to seed and produce beautiful articulate shapes. The genus name comes from the Greek and means a little scale, in reference to the flat, scale-like pods. The species name means from the fields.

PERIOD OF BLOOM: May to September.

PICKING: It is essential to pick these pods while they are still green. Eventually, the green will become yellowish or cream, but when the pods are picked young, before they shed seed, the stems do not acquire a distraught and unkempt configuration.

Limonium carolinianum
and
L. nashii
SEA LAVENDER

COMMON NAMES: sea lavender, marsh rosemary, canker root, lavender thrift, ink root, marsh root, American thrift.

HISTORY: *L. carolinianum* is found on tidal marshes along the east coast of North America. A similar

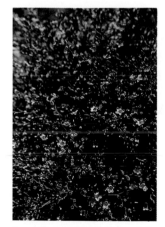

species, *L. nashii*, is found in sea marshes north of the Carolinas. However, in many states it is a protected plant, meaning that picking is prohibited. An option is to grow *L. latifolium* in your own garden. See further historical discussion in Chapter 3.

PERIOD OF BLOOM: July to September.

PICKING: Be sure to pick moderately only where abundant and not prohibited by law. It is a delicate plant that requires careful handling. Use scissors for cutting the stem without pulling. Pick when four-fifths of the spike has opened up. Most flowers open in the heat of the sun.

Linaria vulgaris
BUTTER-AND-EGGS

COMMON NAMES: butter-and-eggs, ranstead, common toadflax, wild snapdragon, brideweed, flax-weed, eggs-and-bacon, yellow

toadflax, impudent lawyer, Jacob's ladder, rancid, wild tobacco, devil's flax, devil's flower, dead men's bones, bread-and-butter, continental weed, gallwort, rabbit-flower.
HISTORY: Originally native to Europe and Asia, *Linaria* has become naturalized in North America, where it grows in fields and waste places, often on disturbed soils (e.g., gravelly parking lots). In many areas, this species is a perennial, but where winters are severe it behaves like its cousin the snapdragon—it survives the winter but dies in the spring. According to Linnaeus, a decoction of this plant in milk was used as a fly poison. In certain folk medicines it was used to treat jaundice and, externally, hemorrhoids. The genus name comes from the Greek meaning linen-like, in reference to its resemblance to flax. *Vulgaris* means common. In England, this plant was also called rambling sailor, wandering sailor, pedlar's

basket and mother of millions. If you would like to entertain and delight little children, pick a flower and squeeze it gently on the sides. The flower will snap as if it were a snapdragon.
PERIOD OF BLOOM: June to October.
PICKING: Although its relative the cultivated snapdragon is too full of moisture to dry by hanging. *Linaria* is drier. When picked while the top flowers are still developing and then dried rapidly, the plant will retain color very well and its shape moderately well. The pods should be picked immediately after flowering.

Lythrum salicaria
PURPLE LOOSESTRIFE

COMMON NAMES: purple loosestrife, spiked willow-herb, long purples, soldiers, purple-grass, willow weed, kill-weed, sagewillow, red Sally, rainbow weed.
HISTORY: Naturalized from Europe, this weed is now found throughout North American swamps, marshes and waterways, where it is beginning to clog passages. Some species of *Lythrum* and varieties of *L. salicaria* are cultivated in gardens for a striking effect. Cultivars found are *roseum superbum* and *tomentosum* with bracts and calyx white-tomentose.

They are propagated by seed and division and survive in any moist soil. The genus name comes from the Greek meaning gore or black blood, in reference to the color of the flower. The species name refers to the willow-like shape of the leaves.
PERIOD OF BLOOM: June through August.
PICKING: To pick *Lythrum*, one should follow the rules for picking spikes. Pick when approximately two-thirds of the spike has opened up. The color of the dried flowers becomes less intense and darker, but the dry flower is still attractive either by itself or in arrangements. The undeveloped top of the spike has a mauve color.

Phragmites australis
COMMON REED

COMMON NAMES: common reed, pole reed, bog reed, Dutch reed, spires, bennels, wild broom corn.
HISTORY: There are over 4,500 species of grasses found throughout the world, and many are use-

ful as decoration. *Phragmites* is found in swampy areas in the United States, Europe and Asia. The genus name comes from the Greek in reference to its hedge-like growth. Calligraphers made quills out of *Phragmites*. In the Soviet Union, it is an important crop because it is a source of cellulose for the manufacture of paper.

Grasses are used for food,

Marshes are magical places and are a source of *Limonium nashii*. But picking should be done conservatively.

Standing ten feet tall, *Phragmites australis* should be picked while it is still young, otherwise it has a tendency to feather out.

Linaria vulgaris, or butter-and-eggs, is a relative of snapdragon and often grows by railroad tracks.

Physalis heterophylla grows in abandoned lots and along roads.

Clematis virginiana pods glistening with morning dew.

forage and decoration. Among the important decorative grasses listed in catalogues are: *Agrostis* (cloud grass), *Aristida* (poverty grass), *Panicum* (panic grass), *Setaria* (foxtail), *Avena* (animated oat), *Festuca* (fescue grass), *Melica* (melic or pearl grass), *Coix* (Job's tears; when it is drying, it has a particularly unpleasant musky odor), *Hordeum* (squirreltail grass) and *Zea* (Indian corn). Many of

Hordeum jubatum

these occur in the wild. Looking for specific grasses is a treasure hunt, and finding grasses for decoration is not difficult at all, for many are nearby: in the garden, on the lawn, in the meadow. Where grasses are undesirable, they are weeds, and often difficult to eradicate.

PERIOD OF BLOOM: July to September.

PICKING: Most grasses should be picked when the flowers are still young—that is, before the seeds form. In some grasses, such as *Phragmites*, seed is not even noticeable. However, if flowers are picked too late, the heads will keep on maturing, and when the seeds form, the spikes will shatter.

Physalis heterophylla
GROUND CHERRY

COMMON NAME: clammy ground cherry.

HISTORY: Native to eastern North America, it is a close relative to *P. peruviana* (husk tomato, Cape

gooseberry, strawberry tomato), which is cultivated for its fruit. *P. heterophylla* is a highly variable species often found in disturbed rich soil. It spreads by seed and roots.

PERIOD OF BLOOM: July to September.

PICKING: Pick as you would cultivated *Physalis*, when the pods are mature.

Plantago major and spp.
PLANTAIN

COMMON NAMES: plantain, dooryard plantain, wayside plantain, round-leaf plantain, broad-leaf plantain, hen-plant, lamb's foot, way-bread, healing-blade, ribgrass, rib-wort.

HISTORY: Indigenous to the north temperate zone, some members of this genus came from Europe

and became naturalized in North America. This species is found in waste places and is considered a weed on lawns. According to Gerard, it was used to treat bleeding ulcers and sores. It was taken internally to ameliorate illnesses in which there was spitting or passing of blood. In Scotland and Russia, the leaves were applied externally as a hemostatic agent. According to some early records, a Negro by the name of Caesar discovered that it can also be effective in treating bites of venomous reptiles and insects. For this discovery, he received a large reward from the South Carolina Assembly. The genus name is from the Latin in reference to the sole of the foot; the plant was found on footpaths.

PERIOD OF BLOOM: May to September.

PICKING: Pick the spikes when they are still in bloom for their green color. Pods may also be useful when bunched in arrangements.

Polygonella articulata
JOINTED KNOTWEED

COMMON NAMES: jointed knotweed, coast knotweed, sand knotweed, coast jointweed.

HISTORY: This annual weed grows on dry sandy soil from the east coast of the United States to the Great Lakes region. It is a beautiful plant that is often found blooming on New England roadsides just before frost.

PERIOD OF BLOOM: Late July to October.

PICKING: The spike should be approximately four-fifths developed when the plant is picked for drying. The plant has virtually no leaves or moisture; it is dry almost

as soon as it is picked. A delicate little plant, it has the gentle appearance of a *Gypsophila* or *Limonium latifolium* when used in arrangements.

Polygonum orientale
SMARTWEED

COMMON NAMES: smartweed, prince's feather, princess feather, kiss-me-over-the-garden-gate, water pepper, biting knotweed.
HISTORY: There are about 150 species in this genus of common weedy plants. *P. orientale* is native to Asia and Australia but has become naturalized in North America. The genus name means that the plant has many knees; it is jointed. Polygonaceae is the buckwheat family. Many species are used medicinally, including *bistorta*, *amphibium*, *barbatum* and *hydropiper*. *Bistorta* has been listed in the pharmacopoeias of Switzerland, France and Russia. In northern countries, it was eaten in the

spring. Because it contains vitamin C, as do other members of the family, it was used to cure gingivitis. *P. persicaria*, called lady's thumb, pinchweed, virgin's pinch (because it was said to have been pinched by the Virgin Mary), was used to treat heart disease and thereby acquired the name hearts-ease. Smartweeds have been used in summer salads. Gerard even suggested that it could be used under a saddle to relieve a horse's discomfort. You should watch out for *P. cuspidatum* (Japanese knotweed or Mexican bamboo). This plant has deep roots, is prolific and is impossible to eradicate. Brought into this country as a foundation plant for Victorian houses and barns, this

weed is still found in areas where there are neither houses nor foundations.
PERIOD OF BLOOM: July to September.
PICKING: All *Polygonum* species should be picked while their blooms are still young. The spike should have opened all the way, but the bloom should not have fully matured. The short and moist species should be dried more quickly and in smaller bunches, because they have a tendency to mold.

Potentilla arguta and spp.
CINQUEFOIL

COMMON NAMES: tall cinquefoil, rough-fruited cinquefoil (*P. recta*).

HISTORY: Found on rocky and dry soil throughout North America, many members of this genus were known for their medicinal uses. That is why the Latin genus name refers to these plants as potent medicines. Gerard enumerated the fantastic list of ailments that this plant supposedly cured: bleeding, diseases of the liver and lungs, all poisons, jaundice and "falling sickness" (epilepsy). *P. arguta* has creamy flowers; the shorter *P. recta* has yellow flowers. *Arguta* means sharp-toothed.
PERIOD OF BLOOM: June to July.
PICKING: Pick either during the last stages of flowering or shortly after the flowers have gone by. Definitely pick while the color of the pods is still green. The color is fast for a long time.

Rhus typhina
SUMAC

COMMON NAMES: staghorn sumac, vinegar tree, American

sumac, Virginia sumac, hairy sumac, velvet sumac.

HISTORY: This American species is found from the east coast to the Midwest. Other *Rhus* species have been used medicinally, some are poisonous, others have economic value. *R. vernix* (Japanese sumac) is poisonous but has been a source of black lacquers in China and Japan. *R. coriaria* is used in tanning fine grades of morocco leather and, in Turkey, in the production of vinegar. *R. anacardium* (Indian cashew nut) has been used for making ink for stamping linen. *R. typhina* was used by American Indians as a stomach medicine. The genus name means reddish. The species name implies that it was used for treating fevers.

PERIOD OF BLOOM: Summer.

PICKING: Pick the tight red clusters (there are various reds, ranging from bright to almost black) before cold weather comes and before chickadees decide to dine on the berries.

Rumex acetosa
and spp.
SORREL

COMMON NAMES: sheep sorrel, green sorrel, sour sorrel, sharp dock. Also note *R. acetosella* (red or common sorrel), *R. altissimus*

(wood dock) and *R. crispus* (wild or yellow dock).

HISTORY: Related to rhubarb, many sorrels are sour and have oxalates (chemical crystalline compounds that are abrasive to the stomach lining) in their leaves. French sorrel and other sorrels are used in soups. Large wild docks are weedy and are found along roads and in marshy areas. The genus name comes from the Latin meaning to suck, implying that sucking on the leaves allays thirst. Native to Asia and Europe, various species have become naturalized in North America.

PERIOD OF BLOOM: March to August.

PICKING: Flowers should be picked while they are developing.

Pods can be picked at various stages of coloration as they turn from green to greenish red to red toward the end of the season. The color stays fast. Late in the season, the brown color is rarely attractive.

Saponaria officinalis
BOUNCING BET

COMMON NAMES: bouncing Bet, soapwort, London pride, bruisewort, Fuller's herb, Boston pink, chimney pink, hedge pink, old-maid's pink, sheepweed, soap

root, world's wonder, sweet Betty, wild Sweet William, lady-by-the-gate, wood's phlox, mock-gilliflower.

HISTORY: Called *Saponaria* because of the scouring quality of the leaves, which were used as soap, it naturalized from Europe and is found along roads and in waste places in North America. In the garden, it is very weedy, spreading by seed and stolons.

PERIOD OF BLOOM: June through August.

PICKING: Pick pods shortly after the plants stop blooming. At this stage, the pods are light and retain a pink tinge reminiscent of the color of the flowers.

Silene antirrhina
and spp.
CATCHFLY

COMMON NAMES: catchfly, sleepy catchfly.

Plumed species of goldenrod (*Solidago*) are good for backgrounds in wreaths and arrangements.

HISTORY: Found in waste places in eastern North America, this plant is perhaps known more for its attractive pods than for its flowers, which open for only a short time in sunshine. Its genus name is derived from the Greek for saliva, in reference to the viscid secretions of many of its species.

PERIOD OF BLOOM: Summer.

PICKING: Pick shortly after the flowers have gone by to retain a greenish-pink color.

Solidago canadensis
and spp.
GOLDENROD

COMMON NAMES: goldenrod, rock goldenrod, yellow top, yellow weed, flower of gold.

HISTORY: This genus contains over 130 species of summer- and autumn-flowering herbs. Most are native to North America; two or three species are native to Europe. Most species cross readily to produce individuals that are difficult to identify except by chromosome analysis. Many species are separated by rather technical distinctions. The genus name comes from either Greek or Latin (depending on the source) and means to make whole or to unite, in reference to its use in healing wounds. The European plants have common names such as woundwort and farewell-summer (when goldenrod blooms, autumn is imminent). Goldenrod has an interesting history associated with its use as a medicine. According to Gerard, fantastic prices were paid in London for the imported dry herb until someone found a native species in a backyard. At this point, the prices dropped precipitously. *S. odora* has leaves that, when crushed, emit a fragrance of anise. But other species also have fragrant leaves that give off pleasant fragrances, including lemon. They can be used in tea, and were so utilized during the American Revolution. This plant has been much maligned as a cause of hay fever and other late-summer allergies. However, the plant is pollinated by butterflies and other insects and not very much by the wind. Thus, it is not the pollen of goldenrod that is the culprit, but the pollen of ragweed (*Ambrosia* spp.), which blooms simultaneously and occupies a similar niche.

PERIOD OF BLOOM: Late summer and early autumn.

PICKING: The most useful species for drying are those that have plumes—*rugosa, canadensis, neglecta, uniligulata, arguta, juncea, glaberrima* and *nemoralis*. The least useful species are those that have flat tops, such as *rigida, ohionensis* and *riddellii*. The reason for this difference is that the plumed species open after they are picked and will keep their attractive yellow color. The flat-top species do not retain color and do not dry well. *Solidago* occupies many environmental niches. It can be found on saltwater and freshwater marshes as well as on dry fields. In order to preserve color and shape, *Solidago* should be picked when it is only one-third or less developed. When it is found on marshland, it should be picked just as the buds begin to open at the bottom. The more moisture the plant has, the more likely it will keep on maturing after it is picked. Thus, the decision on when to pick is critical. The early-flowering species have a tendency to have less color when dry. The late-flowering species, the fall-flowering especially, tend to retain their beautiful golden color. This is an important and valuable filler for both arrangements and wreaths.

Spiraea tomentosa
STEEPLEBUSH

COMMON NAMES: steeplebush, hardhack, silver-leaf, white cap, meadow-sweet, poor man's soap, spice-hardhack, rosy-bush.

HISTORY: This shrub is usually found in swampy or low ground from the east coast of the United States to the Midwest. It is related to the white American meadow-sweet or Quaker Lady and to bridal wreath (*Spiraea × vanhouttei*, a hybrid of *S. cantoniensis* and *S. trilobata*), which is a popular landscaping shrub (that also may be dried). According to some sources, the genus name is derived from Greek in reference to the twisting of pods in some species.

According to other sources, the Greek word *speiraira*, "to wind," refers to the utilization of *Spiraea* as a plant for making garlands.
PERIOD OF BLOOM: July to September.
PICKING: This is an unusual spike in that it blooms from the top down. Therefore, it is important to pick the flower before the terminal panicles mature.

Trifolium agrarium and *T. arvense* CLOVER

COMMON NAMES: *T. agrarium:* hop clover. *T. arvense:* rabbit-foot clover, stone clover, poverty grass, bottle grass, dogs-and-cats, pussies, pussy-cats.
HISTORY: Cultivated clovers are important forage and cover crops that are propagated by seed. There are over 300 species of *Trifolium*, and most are native to the north temperate zone. Both of the above species are now found in the United States but are native

to Europe. In the wild, they are found in waste places from the east coast to the Midwest. The genus name is, of course, derived from the Latin in reference to its three leaves.
PERIOD OF BLOOM: May to September.
PICKING: Flowers should be

picked shortly after they open. In the case of *T. agrarium*, the color is best preserved when the flowers are young. In the case of *T. arvense*, the delicate heads, if picked early, are less prone to shattering.

Verbena hastata BLUE VERVAIN

COMMON NAMES: blue vervain, false vervain, wild hyssop, American vervain, purvain, iron-weed.
HISTORY: Many of the species belonging to this genus and found in the wild are native to the United States and Canada. They grow in moist, marshy freshwater areas and often in waste places. The genus name is from the Latin, according to Pliny, in reference to the Holy Herb of the Druids. (Some sources trace it to the Celtic *ferfaen*.) Supposedly, it was used for many ills and to heal wounds. In the south of England, rue and vervain were reputed to be witches' plants. In other places, vervain, in combination with dill, hung on the entrance door, was supposed to deliver one from witches. In ancient times, branches of vervain, to signify war, were carried by ambassadors who defied the enemy. In Germany, coming to signify the god of war and thunder, it was used to ward off lightning and storms.

American Indians used the plant to stem bleeding. *Hastata* means spear-like.
PERIOD OF BLOOM: June to September.
PICKING: Since the spike is constantly blooming, pick when approximately two-thirds of the flowers have bloomed. The color will not stay, but the form is attractive nevertheless.

Vicia cracca VETCH

COMMON NAMES: tufted vetch, cow vetch, blue vetch, bird vetch, tinegrass, cat peas, Canada peas.
HISTORY: Many species in this genus are used for food, forage

and green manure. Most are vigorous and resilient in any kind of soil. Although native to Eurasia, *Vicia* has become naturalized in the United States. In the wild, it is found in waste places. The genus name is from the Latin *vincio*, to bind, in reference to its tendrils. Gerard suggested that "when applied with honey before the act" it hindered conception.
PERIOD OF BLOOM: June to August.
PICKING: Pick when two-thirds of the flowers have opened up, and dry rapidly, because the spike is full of moisture. If dried slowly, the color fades.

Collector's Guide for Gathering in the Wild

PAGE NUMBER	GENUS	SPECIES	COMMON NAME	HEIGHT	PART USED
119	Antennaria	neglecta	pussy-toes	10″	flower
119	Artemisia	stelleriana	dusty miller	18″	flower
119	Asclepias	syriaca	milkweed	4′	pod
119–122	Campanula	rapunculoides	creeping bellflower	3′	pod
122	Capsella	bursa-pastoris	shepherd's purse	18″	pod
122	Carex	lurida	sedge	3′	pod
122–123	Cephalanthus	occidentalis	button bush	20′	pod
123	Cirsium	vulgare	bull thistle	5′	flower
123	Clematis	virginiana	virgin's bower	9′	pod
123	Coronilla	varia	crown vetch	3′	flower
124	Daucus	carota	Queen Anne's lace	3′	flower and pod
124	Echium	vulgare	viper's bugloss	3′	flower
124	Epilobium	angustifolium	fireweed	5′	flower and pod
122	Eriophorum	virginicum	cotton grass	2′	flower
124–125	Eupatorium	perfoliatum	boneset	4′	flower
125	Eupatorium	purpureum	Joe-Pye weed	7′	flower
125–128	Gnaphalium	obtusifolium	sweet everlasting	2′	flower
128	Hieracium	aurantiacum	hawkweed, orange	20″	flower
128	Hieracium	villosum	hawkweed, yellow	20″	flower
128	Iris	versicolor	iris	3′	pod
128–129	Juncus	canadensis	rush	3′	pod
129	Lechea	racemulosa	pinweed	9″	flower
129	Lepidium	campestre	pepper grass	2′	pod
129–130	Limonium	carolinianum	sea lavender	18″	flower
129–130	Limonium	nashii	sea lavender	18″	flower
130	Linaria	vulgaris	butter-and-eggs	2′	flower
130	Lythrum	salicaria	purple loosestrife	5′	flower
130–136	Phragmites	australis	common reed	10′	flower
136	Physalis	heterophylla	clammy ground cherry	3′	pod
136	Plantago	major	plantain	18″	flower
136–137	Polygonella	articulata	jointed knotweed	18″	flower
137	Polygonum	orientale	smartweed	3′	flower
137	Potentilla	arguta	cinquefoil, tall	3′	pod
137–138	Rhus	typhina	sumac	15′	pod
138	Rumex	acetosa	sheep sorrel	18″	flower and pod
138	Saponaria	officinalis	bouncing Bet	3′	pod
138–140	Silene	antirrhina	sleepy catchfly	2′	pod
140	Solidago	canadensis	goldenrod	4′	flower
140–141	Spiraea	tomentosa	steeplebush	4′	flower
129	Thlaspi	arvense	field pennycress	2′	pod
141	Trifolium	agrarium	hop clover	20″	flower
141	Trifolium	arvense	rabbit-foot clover	10″	flower
141	Verbena	hastata	blue vervain	4′	flower
141	Vicia	cracca	cow vetch	3′	flower

A sedge by the roadside.

6
Designing with Everlastings

After the last fall frost, our home, the everlasting shop and three barns are filled with thousands of stems of dried materials. The array of colors, shapes and textures is indeed beautiful. The most recently harvested materials stand out because of their brilliance, but dried materials from years past, which have not yet found their way into a wreath or basket, are equally lovely. Sometimes their colors have softened into shades that are invaluable for any designer's palette. If you are fortunate enough to have beamed ceilings, you may be content to let your everlastings hang handsomely from pegs and nails and never rearrange your harvest. But if you spend any time at all

enjoying the colors and shapes, you will no doubt be tempted to play with some of the everlastings, coaxing them into wreaths and containers.

Our initial interest in dried flowers was focused on the horticulture of the plants themselves. For several years, we were content to bundle our everlastings into simple nosegays for ourselves, and then for gifts, and finally for a growing number of customers. As our knowledge of plant material increased, so did our interest in the design possibilities of everlastings. Now, after many years of growing and harvesting everlastings, we have the luxury of designing with a rich assortment of plants. But we began with only a few varieties and even the beginning gardener can raise enough material to design wreaths and arrangements after one season. We also like to encourage both growers and non-growers to go out and gather in the wild. Roadsides and meadows offer hundreds of handsome plant forms. Once you begin to take notice, you are likely to see flowers, grasses, pods and weeds that you can incorporate into beautiful designs.

We also offer this bit of encouragement to new gardeners and designers: There are no strict rules and limitations for designing with everlastings. There are seemingly endless ways of as-

sembling dried materials into pleasing forms. Each grouping of colors and textures will have its own unique flavor, with some, no doubt, more pleasing to you than others. You should approach your designing as an adventure in learning about color, form, structure, texture and the qualities of light. Never make any assumptions about what materials will work with other materials until you have actually put them together. The resonance that is created by juxtaposing one flower against another will often be surprising. We often compare flower arranging to composing a piece of music. One note, one flower, takes its meaning in the context of other notes, other flowers. The designs can be harmonious, lyrical, dramatic, sumptuous, spare, symmetrical or abstract.

Perhaps the greatest pleasure we experience from working with everlastings comes from the fact that we are both growers and designers. It is hard to imagine that growing flowers alone would be enough if we were not to have the fun of trying to work our harvests into arrangements. Conversely, it is difficult to imagine that it would be satisfying simply to be given dried material with which to work. The greatest satisfaction in designing comes from having learned about the plants, having watched them develop from seeds to harvest, or having found some wonderful new dried materials in the wild. When we discover new plants in the wild, we always try to research the plant's identity and learn about its growing habits. We often end up introducing a few samples of wild plants into our cultivated gardens and fields.

With all of this in mind, we urge you to grow, gather and work with materials that you have come to know and enjoy. There will be pleasures and surprises enough for a lifetime.

The following sections have been prepared to help you with a number of design projects. Use these suggestions as a point of departure. They should help you with basic techniques and design ideas. Throughout the chapter, we will refer to plants by their most common names. At the end of the book there is a complete cross-reference of common and botanical names of the everlasting plants mentioned in this volume.

FIGURE 1

Making an Herbal Wreath

Both floral and everlasting wreaths have been made for many centuries, so it is perhaps appropriate to begin the design section with the fashioning of an herbal wreath. In this case we are planning to use the wreath as a decorative piece, but different civilizations have used wreaths not only as decoration but symbolically to honor their heroes, to commemorate their deceased, to symbolize eternity, to welcome visitors and to indicate position and power.

While many materials have been used to construct wreaths, we will focus on some special dried materials that either a grower or a gatherer might want to use. When speaking of dried material, we generally divide the plants into categories of filler material or background and detailing or accent material. The first category is made up of plant material that has a natural fullness and hence can be used to build body or mass into a design. Wreaths generally need to be made from a goodly portion of filler material so that the final piece has shape, dimension and body. Some of the most useful fillers for wreaths include sea lavender, Silver King artemisia, goldenrod, white or rose achillea, statice, baby's

breath, lady's mantle and eucalyptus. One could add a number of other plants to the list, remembering that it is the form of the material that makes it suitable for the design.

The list of dried material used for detailing or accenting is likewise long, but for the sake of brevity, let us name a few such as helichrysum, globe amaranth, acroclinium and ammobium.

Growers who wish to have enough materials for designing should pay some attention to the proportions of their gardens, since it takes a larger amount of filler material to make not only a wreath but also a container arrangement. A combination of cultivated plants and plants gathered in the wild can amply supply the designer.

We have chosen to explain the process of making a wreath with the use of Silver King artemisia as a background, because it is easy to grow and pleasant to work with. It is also an attractive neutral background to which color can be applied easily.

FIGURE 1 At Hedgehog Hill, we fashion all of our wreaths on crimped wire frames, weaving all of the wreath from the dried material. There are other methods of making herbal wreaths, such as

FIGURE 2

FIGURE 3

covering Styrofoam or straw backs, but we prefer the crafting of wreaths entirely from dried material. Thus we will begin the step-by-step explanation.

FIGURE 2 Choose a circle of crimped wire to correspond to the size of wreath you wish to make. Keep in mind that an 8″-diameter ring will result in a wreath measuring approximately 12″ across. A wreath done on a 10″ ring will be approximately 14″ when finished, and one on a 14″ ring will be about 18″. First wrap the ring tightly with green or brown floral tape. This covering will prevent the dried material from slipping.

FIGURE 3 Begin with the background material, done here in Silver King artemisia, and break the stems into 3″–4″ lengths, working down the stem of each piece so that you are using all of the material available. When the stem gets too large

and stiff, discard it and go to the next piece. One kind of background material may be used, or you may use various materials in combination. In making a silver artemisia wreath, you could use only the Silver King, or you could mix it with other varieties of artemisia, such as wormwood, mugwort or Silver Mound. Combinations can produce a pleasant blending of grays and silvers.

FIGURE 4 Shape the 3″–4″ lengths into a fan, holding the ends of the pieces between the thumb and fingers of one hand. Try to shape the fan as broadly as possible. Imagine that you are making a protractor out of the dried background. The fan should be full and even.

FIGURE 5 With your other hand, take a 12″ length of flexible wire—we suggest 28 gauge— and wrap the fan at its base, being certain to maintain the shape with your other hand. Use

FIGURE 6

FIGURE 7

FIGURE 4

FIGURE 5

about a third of the wire to wrap the fan, leaving the remaining length free for the next step.

FIGURE 6 Place the fan on the face of the crimped ring, directly in the center of the front, and continue to wrap the wire around the fan and the ring. Wrap tightly until the fan is firmly attached to the ring. If you feel that the fan is at all loose, use a second wire to attach it securely.

FIGURE 7 Turn the ring over and examine the way in which you have positioned your first fan. Make certain that this fan and all remaining fans are tied onto the middle front of the ring. Remember that you are forming not only the outside of the wreath but the inner circle as well. If your fans are directed to the outer part of the ring, the center circle of the finished wreath may be large and ungraceful.

FIGURE 8 Using your background material,

shape the next fan and position it over the first, overlapping slightly. As a rule of thumb, we tend to tie fans to every other crimped section of the ring. Now you have begun the series of steps that you will follow until the background of the wreath is done.

FIGURE 9 Continue to shape, wrap and wire the fans onto the crimped ring. There are several things to keep in mind when making the background. The size, length and shaping of your first fan should be repeated consistently throughout the making of the wreath. If you begin with one size fan and increase or decrease the size as you work around the ring, your wreath will not be smooth and symmetrical. If you are a beginner, work slowly at first in order to establish uniform parts for a well-balanced wreath.

FIGURE 10 When you have succeeded in ty-

FIGURE 8

FIGURE 9

FIGURE 10

FIGURE 11

ing in the last fan, your wreath should be pleasingly round and full. It should also be firmly tied to the ring, with no fans feeling as if they are loose. If any parts of the wreath feel loose, it is best to go back and rewrap the individual fans before continuing. Now you are ready to begin the most exciting part of your work.

FIGURE 11 Choose the herbs and everlastings that you will use to highlight your wreath. For this design we are using apricot statice, plumed celosia, hydrangea, blue salvia and helichrysum. Remember that a wreath may be either heavily colored or done in soft and subtle colors. The background may be completed with a few highlights or with abundant additional material. The choice of color and degree of decoration is a personal one, and there are endless successful solutions in the design of herbal wreaths. Begin

with one or two everlastings that have strong stems. Simply break off the material, leaving a 3″–4″ stem. With one hand, gently lift the background material, and insert the stem of the accent piece, weaving the stem into the base so that it is tightly caught in one of the fans. Work all the way around your wreath with any one material at a time, shaping and balancing the highlights as you go.

FIGURE 12 Try to avoid placing accent pieces in symmetrical patterns, as this often results in a wreath that is static in design. Remember, too, that you are designing the overall wreath, not just the center of the front of the wreath. Thus you should place the pieces of color in varying positions around the wreath, sometimes near the center of the circle, sometimes near the outside and sometimes in the middle of the wreath.

FIGURE 14

FIGURE 15

FIGURE 12

FIGURE 13

Even if your accent pieces are few and subtle in color and texture, they should have the overall effect of being woven into the wreath, not dotted precisely around the background.

FIGURE 13 When you come to adding smaller accent pieces, it is often best to wrap these everlastings onto a small floral pick. Picks are also used for materials that have insubstantial stems.

FIGURE 14 Hold the flowers, pods or grasses close to the floral pick and carefully wrap the small piece of wire around the stems. If the weather is very dry, handle the material gently so that you do not snap off any flower heads. Small accent pieces are most effective if used in clusters of two to four to a pick.

FIGURE 15 The flowers on the picks are inserted into the wreath in the same manner as the natural stems. The picks simply act as strong substitutes for holding, pushing and securely placing materials into the background.

FIGURE 16 When the face of the wreath is fully designed, it will look as if the accents and the background are integrated naturally. It is not essential to add accent pieces to the entire wreath. Some successful designs are done with accents in crescent shapes on the top or on one side. You will no doubt have fun in discovering the many ways to finish a wreath.

FIGURE 17 When you have added all of your final color, fashion a small hanger out of a piece of wire and attach the hanger to the back of the wreath. Then hang the wreath up for a final critique. Look at the work both close up and from a distance. You will undoubtedly see one or two spots you wish to adjust. Now you have a wreath to enjoy for years.

FIGURE 16

FIGURE 17

Sea lavender, plumed and crested celosia, statice,
ageratum, red salvia, globe amaranth, helichrysum.

Winter rye.

Sea lavender, ambrosia, rabbit-tail grass,
animated oats, hydrangea, statice.

Sea lavender, oregano, lavender, hydrangea,
lady's mantle, baby's breath, eryngium.

Silver King artemisia, goldenrod, pearly everlasting, chives, oregano, lavender, golden yarrow, winter rye, eryngium.

There is no end to the kind of materials that can be fashioned into herbal wreaths. The background of this one, very Victorian in feeling, was done with goldenrod and tansy. All of the accents are in quiet tones of beige, cream and wine. We added matricaria, hydrangea (in its creamy stage), the wine-colored blossoms of oregano and finally the pods of nigella.

The red, white and blue design was fashioned on a Silver King artemisia background. Reds are from the addition of plumed celosia and helichrysum. White comes from the use of both white statice and white helichrysum. The blue is the very useful blue salvia. Notice how important it is to weave these elements throughout the face of the wreath.

In this complicated wreath, made by a very experienced designer, all of the materials were woven into the original fans to create the overall effect of a wreath in apricot hues. Nothing was added after the original tying of the fans. This wreath takes considerable practice to make, because one does not have the chance to correct for any unevenness in the shaping. It does suggest, however, that a background may be made with several materials and then some final accents may be added. Dried materials include sea lavender, hydrangea, globe amaranth, ageratum, statice and helichrysum.

The techniques that are explained in this section on wreath making should stand you in good stead no matter what materials you decide to use. This wreath, made with hundreds of pods of nigella and a small amount of sea lavender, was constructed in exactly the same manner as all of our designs. We have found that the overlapping-fan technique is applicable to an endless number of materials and is thus a very useful technique to learn.

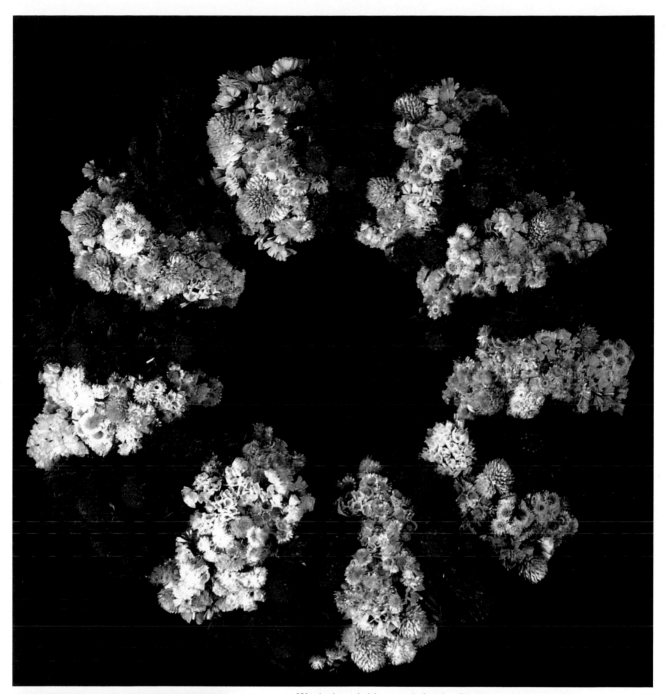

We designed this wreath for the Christmas holidays, using alternating fans of red material and white material. We sometimes call this our candy-cane wreath, and it too is constructed exactly like the wreath explained in detail earlier. The red materials include sea lavender, red plumed and crested celosia, ageratum, globe amaranth and helichrysum. The white fans were made from white yarrow, white statice, white globe amaranth, ammobium and pearly everlasting.

Wreaths can also be used nicely with candles. The background of artemisia and pearly everlasting is accented with white ammobium and blue globe thistle. We use scentless candles with our herbal wreaths. Artificially scented candles detract from the natural fragrances of the everlastings.

Silver King artemisia, hydrangea, chives, blue salvia, globe amaranth, blue globe thistle, helichrysum.

Sea lavender, lady's mantle, eucalyptus moorei nana, black sorghum, lavender, sorrel, fragrant flowering garlic, hydrangea, bittersweet, helichrysum.

Silver King artemisia, eucalyptus cinerea, hydrangea, sedum, black sorghum, Chinese lantern, sand-dried zinnias.

Sea lavender, hydrangea, chives, blue salvia, plumed celosia, helichrysum.

Mountain mint, oregano, hydrangea, chives, delphinium, blue globe thistle, sand-dried zinnias.

Arrangements of everlastings complement traditional decor, *above*,
and a country setting, *right*.

Silver King artemisia, Silver Mound artemisia, pearly everlasting, hydrangea, blue globe thistle and helichrysum.

Sea lavender, statice, plumed celosia, goldenrod, wild meadow grasses and helichrysum.

Silver King artemisia, Silver Mound artemisia, hydrangea, blue globe thistle and larkspur.

Sea lavender, rose statice, crested celosia, pink and magenta globe amaranth and helichrysum.

Plumed and crested celosia, dock, sweet wormwood, sage, ambrosia, Joe-Pye weed, golden yarrow, orange marigolds and globe centaurea.

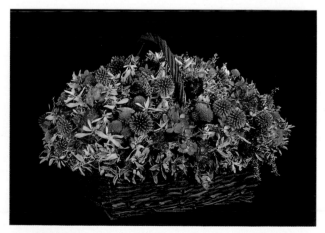

Silver King artemisia, hydrangea, blue globe thistle, pink globe amaranth, rose and burgundy helichrysum, and rhodanthe.

Eucalyptus, hydrangea, oregano and pink and blue larkspur.

OVERLEAF Sea lavender, goldenrod, marjoram, ambrosia, matricaria, plumed and crested celosia, golden ageratum and helichrysum.

Sea lavender, ambrosia, statice, hydrangea, globe amaranth and animated oats.

Silver King artemisia, apricot and rose statice, hydrangea and bull thistle.

FIGURE 1

Hats with Flowers and Ribbons

Broad-brimmed hats with a band of everlastings and flowing ribbons, narrow-brimmed hats with a grosgrain ribbon and a touch of everlastings, visors with a small band of grasses and herbs—these are but a few ways in which hats can be designed for wearing or for decorating. The material from which the hat is made can vary as much as the material used in its decoration. Straw hats, both natural and in colors, have a certain country feeling. For wearing to weddings and summer lawn parties, you might choose hats made of linen or organdy. To demonstrate one popular idea, we will follow the step-by-step design of a wide-brimmed straw

hat. This should suggest a number of ways in which to adapt the idea.

FIGURE 1: Assemble the tools and materials that will be needed for the whole project. They include the wide-brimmed hat, enough 21-gauge wire to encircle the crown of the hat, floral tape, scissors, an assortment of ribbons to complement the colors of the everlastings and the selection of dried materials you will use in the design. The everlastings that we selected for this demonstration include sea lavender, various tones of apricot statice, crested and plumed celosia, Joe-Pye weed, matricaria and rose, burgundy and apricot shades of helichrysum.

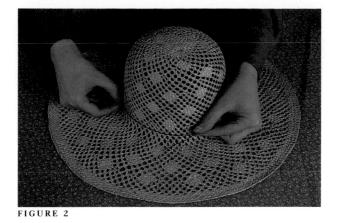

FIGURE 2

FIGURE 3

FIGURE 2　Using a length of 21-gauge wire, fashion a circle around the crown of the hat. Twist the ends of the wire so that the circle is fitted loosely to the crown. It is important that the wire circle be loose enough to allow for the bulk that will be added from the clusters of dried material. When the floral material is complete, the wire ring should sit completely down on the crown.

FIGURE 3　Once the wire circle is formed, cover it entirely with green or brown floral tape. This tape makes it easier to fasten the dried material securely to the wire. You can also use pipe cleaners to make the ring around the crown, and in that case, it is not necessary to cover the cleaners with floral tape, as the fuzzy finish of the cleaners will hold the dried clusters in place. Either wire or pipe cleaners will work well as a base.

FIGURE 4　Begin the design by choosing two or three kinds of dried materials and breaking the stems into 2″–3″ lengths. Then shape the stems into small fan-shaped clusters. The clusters should not be too large, as the material will build rather quickly on the crown of the hat, and you are trying to design a floral band that is graceful, but not bulky. Depending on the size of the hat, both its crown and brim, one should make a judgment about the fullness of the floral band. This may take some practice, but you will no doubt see some pleasing relationship in scale very early on in your work.

FIGURE 5　Cut a 4″–5″ length of floral tape and wrap the ends of the dried material a couple of turns, so that the stems are held in place.

With the remaining length of tape, attach the cluster of flowers onto the wire circle. The dried material should be secured on the top of

FIGURE 4

FIGURE 5

FIGURE 6

FIGURE 7

the wire circle, allowing it to lie flat on the brim of the hat once the band is complete.

FIGURE 6-7 Continue fashioning small fan-shaped clusters of the dried materials and overlap the clusters to form a delicate band on the wire frame. Vary the choice of materials in each of the fans in such a way that whatever colors and textures you are using are woven in an interesting manner around the crown of the hat. If you simply repeat the same materials in each fan, the final design may be rather static and uninteresting.

FIGURE 8 After attaching several fans, try the circle on the hat to evaluate the size and design. This fitting will allow you to see how the colors are working and how well the ring is fitting with the material attached. Repeat this fitting several times in the design process, so that you can adjust colors, shaping or the size of the wire

ring if necessary before the floral band is finished.

FIGURE 9 Continue to shape and attach the clusters of dried materials until the band is complete. The final two clusters have to be wrapped in carefully so that there is no noticeable spacing between the first and the last cluster of material. Now place the band on the hat and turn the hat around to check for continuity of texture, color and form. If there are places where you feel that extra color or fullness is needed, you can add a few details or sprigs by tucking in dried material with a spot of hot glue to hold the pieces in place.

FIGURE 10 You are now ready to choose ribbons to finish the design. The lengths of the ribbons can vary somewhat, but they should be in proportion to the size of the hat. In this design, we have used 2¼ yards of each color. This length allows us to tie attractive bows and

FIGURE 10

FIGURE 11

FIGURE 8

FIGURE 9

leave long streamers. We suggest anywhere from four to eight different pieces of ribbon, depending on the colors, widths and materials. This design uses a combination of grosgrain, velvet, lace and satin. The ribbons are tied in a group; the bows are carefully separated and spread into a butterfly shape, and the ends of the streamers are all cut at an angle.

FIGURE 11   It is easiest to place the ribbons under the floral band by bending the crown of the hat and slipping the bow under the band so that the knot of the ribbons rests just above the flowers. You may need to readjust the shape of the bows and the streamers once the ribbons are in position. Now your hat is ready for wearing or hanging.

It is interesting to use dried materials to create a natural-colored band around straw hats, as we did in this case with sea lavender and matricaria. The plume of squirreltail grass resembles a natural feather.

Many combinations of colors and ribbons can be used. Lighter colors and pastel ribbons will be more reminiscent of springtime; deeper colors with grosgrain and velvets have a darker fall-like or wintery feeling. If you are using the hats for interior decorating, you may simply change the ribbons to suit the seasons and thus create several different effects with the same basic hat and floral design.

Hearts Made of Flowers

Heart-shaped wreaths are interesting to design and make, if not for every decor or occasion, then for some special times and situations.

The open-heart wreaths are done in much the same way that wreaths are designed. The full-heart forms were originally designed at our farm, and their production is both time-consuming and quite exacting. The very small heart-shaped ornaments were done one Christmas season and displayed on our tree along with sachets of fragrant potpourri. These designs are offered only as suggestions for the grower or designer; there are many materials that can be used to execute the shapes.

FIGURE 1

FIGURE 2

Floral Pins: Boutonnieres and Corsages

FIGURE 1   The techniques and tools needed for designing a floral pin, be it a boutonniere or corsage, are the same. The difference in design rests primarily in the scale of the piece. The boutonniere is traditionally smaller with a simple ribbon; the corsage is larger with a more elaborate ribbon or double bow. This brief description should assist in the design of either. Further examples are shown in the following section on wedding ideas.

FIGURE 2   Assemble your dried materials, floral tape, cutting tools and ribbon. Since the floral pin is quite small, it is best to make a choice of a few dried materials that will blend well, using one or two elements for the background and one or two accent colors and shapes. For this pin, we will work with Silver King artemisia, baby's breath, myrtle and helichrysum.

FIGURE 3   Working with a few sprigs of artemisia, shape the background by using the natural curve of the foliage. Once you have decided on the shape, hold the stems firmly between the thumb and fingers of one hand.

FIGURE 4   Next, add the baby's breath to build the background and give it a softer texture.

FIGURE 5

FIGURE 6

FIGURE 3

FIGURE 4

Once again, cluster all the stems together to hold the shape of the arrangement.

FIGURE 5   If you wish to secure the background stems at this point, wrap the grouping with a small strip of floral tape. You are now ready to arrange the accents with the helichrysum and myrtle, keeping in mind that flower accents are best used in uneven numbers. The helichrysums, both white and gold, are shaped and woven into place with the myrtle at the base of the form.

FIGURE 6   Now, with everything in position, hold the assemblage with one hand and secure the stems in place with a strip of floral tape. Begin by wrapping the tape nearest the flower heads and continue to wrap the stems by pulling the tape gently on a bias all the way down the stems (about an inch or two) until the whole wrapping comes to a gentle taper. The tapered

point may then be carefully shaped by hand into a curve.

FIGURE 7   When the arrangement is finished, the background forms the larger outer shape, with the accents constituting the smaller linear interest, leading the eye down to the base of the arrangement where the ribbon will be placed.

FIGURE 8   The ribbons used to make the single or double bow are best made of a delicate narrow material. One can use picots, velvets, satins or lace. Fashion a single bow from one color or, as in this example, a double bow, picking up the white and gold of the helichrysum. The bow is attached to the base of the floral pin with a piece of thin wire (26 or 28 gauge) or with a drop of hot glue.

Now you need only add the corsage or boutonniere pin, which you can purchase from any floral supply store.

FIGURE 7

FIGURE 8

Everlastings for Weddings

The year-round availability of everlastings makes them ideally suited to wedding design, especially during seasons when fresh flowers are not in bloom, or when imported flowers are scarce and costly. When mixed with fragrant herbal everlastings, such as matricaria, lavender and the various artemisias, wedding designs have a delicate fragrance that lasts for many years. Since there are everlastings in nearly every color imaginable, it is possible to design for the equally numerous colors of bridal costumes. There is even the possibility of having green in everlasting weddings, using myrtle, ambrosia, sweet wormwood and pressed ferns.

Many couples choose everlastings for their wedding flowers because of the beauty and fragrance of the dried materials, but more importantly because the various wedding pieces may be kept for years after the event. Individual items may be displayed as they were originally designed, or the elements of the wedding may be woven into an herbal wreath that will remain both a beautiful and a symbolic reminder of the special day.

Weddings may be as lavishly or as simply designed as one wishes, and the use of material may be varied accordingly. If one chooses a simple country-style wedding, then the bouquets, boutonnieres and basket arrangements may be done in herbs and grasses to resemble the natural landscape. If the wedding is more traditional or formal, then more intricate bouquets may be made up with dried herbs and flowers in profusion. Some couples choose to have altar and temple pieces; some have reception tables decorated with dried arrangements which they can give as gifts to special family members and friends. Small children who participate in the ceremonies can carry baskets filled with dried potpourri to be thrown in lieu of rice. Young girls may also choose to wear bands of everlastings with small ribbon streamers. Pillars, pews and other appropriate architectural structures may be decorated with garlands of everlastings and fragrant herbs.

We are going to take a brief look in this section at some of the more usual wedding designs, and comment on the use of materials and construction of the pieces.

The bridal bouquet can be made up in many sizes and shapes, depending on the size of the bouquet holder, shown separately in the section on tools and supplies on page 185. The materials used in this bouquet are listed below in the order

in which they were placed into the floral foam at the base of the holder. The bouquet was fashioned following the steps used in traditional basket arranging which we described in detail earlier in the chapter. The background was formed with Silver King artemisia. Then the green-gray leaves of lamb's ears were added to give a graceful shape and to expand the shape of the background. The color was then added with rose and apricot statice, burgundy cockscomb and corresponding shades of helichrysum, with additional creamy-white helichrysum put in final positions to accent the color and to coordinate with the ivory wedding gown. The baby's breath was added last in a soft airy layer over the background, to soften and add gracefulness to the final bouquet. While this bouquet was made in a round shape, one could as well fashion a crescent or a cascading bouquet, using longer stems and the leaf shapes of lamb's ears, myrtle or ferns. The ribbons of velvet, satin and lace were attached to the base of the bouquet holder. Their colors were chosen to coordinate with the bridal gown and the attendants' dresses.

When bridal bouquets are made with everlastings, the brides are usually reluctant to toss the finished pieces, so we offer a suggestion for the tossing bouquet. This is a much smaller and simpler bouquet, done in the same colors and materials as the formal arrangement. The materials are held together and shaped into a small

nosegay, and the stems are wrapped with floral tape, until the whole nosegay tapers to a small point, the wrapped stems giving the bride a place to grasp the arrangement. In this sample, we have added a series of lace bows and ribbons around the base of the everlastings, to serve as a frame for the flowers. One could also use small ribbons for streamers if desired. This tossing bouquet becomes a welcome keepsake, and it is sturdy enough so that it can be thrown and caught and still stay intact.

Some brides choose to wear floral hair bands,

which may vary greatly in size and complexity of material used. The hair pieces may be full circles or partial bands, depending on the way in which the bride wears her hair. This sample shown is a full circle, designed to be worn over a simple

veil. The hair band was fashioned in much the same manner as the herbal wreath described in detail earlier in the chapter, with some small changes in the beginning stages of construction. Rather than starting with a rigid wire frame, which would be too heavy and unresponsive to work with, we fashion a light flexible circle with pipe cleaners, adjusting the circle to the size of the wearer's head. The clusters of dried material are then shaped and added step by step to the ring with floral tape. It is important to evaluate the scale of the head piece, because you do not want a wreath on the top of the head, but rather a hair band that sits in proportion to the head, the hairstyle and any veil that may be used. This model is wearing a floral piece made from Silver King artemisia and lamb's ears to coordinate with the bridal bouquet. Accents of apricot and rose statice are also used, but the helichrysum was thought to be too heavy for the design, and we chose instead the smaller and softer flowers of ivory matricaria and a final overlay of baby's breath.

The bouquets for the wedding attendants are usually smaller in scale than the bridal bouquet, and are designed both to coordinate and to contrast slightly with the bride's arrangement. The colors for the wedding, however, are governed by the material of the attendants' costumes. In this example, the women in the wedding party were wearing dresses of deep burgundy. The bridal bouquet used this color as an accent, and the attendants' bouquets were designed with this color and accompanying colors without the shapes of the lamb's ears or the baby's breath, so that there is a special difference

between the bouquets. The attendants' bouquets were fashioned in holders similar to, but smaller than, the bridal holder, and the materials were inserted in the following order. The background was done in artemisia and creamy matricaria. Color was then added with apricot and burgundy statice and the soft mauve color from Joe-Pye weed. The final accents were done with rose, apricot and burgundy helichrysum, but not with white helichrysum, which was reserved for the bridal bouquet.

This small hair piece could be worn by any of the members of the bridal party or fashioned a bit smaller for a child's head. The materials were attached in very small clusters to the bar of a simple hair comb. We used very fine pieces of wire (28 or 30 gauge), and then the tiny helichrysum accents were put in place with a dot of hot glue. The dried materials are artemisia, matricaria, very small leaves of lamb's ears and the smallest helichrysum.

Attendants in this wedding wore wide-brimmed hats decorated with everlastings and ribbons. The materials in the design are the same as the everlastings in the attendants' bouquets. The ribbons are of lace, velvet, satin and grosgrain in an assortment of colors to coordinate with the flowers and dresses. Details for making decorated hats were given earlier in the chapter. We also suggest that wedding hats may be done in linen, cotton, organdy or a delicate mesh fabric.

Boutonnieres for the groom and the men in the wedding party are typically made up with the same dried materials as those for the bride and her attendants. The examples shown are three different design solutions.

This one is made from Silver King artemisia, the pods of rue, apricot statice and burgundy helichrysum (left).

The background is sea lavender, and the colors are provided by red crested celosia and rose helichrysum. The small white flowers are ammobium (right).

The background is sea lavender, with accents of matricaria and helichrysum. Detailed instructions on how to fashion boutonnieres and corsages can be found earlier in this chapter.

The techniques for constructing bouton- nieres and corsages are similar, the basic differ- ence being the scale and complexity of the materials used. With corsages, we tend to use one or two backgrounds and a larger number of accents. The ribbons are often fuller, and in some cases we use contrasting ribbon colors. This corsage was fashioned with artemisia and baby's breath in the background. Then we added blue statice and soft pink globe amaranth and helichrysum. The blue and white ribbons were chosen to tie in the everlasting colors and to coordinate with the mother's dress of soft blue.

The artemisia and baby's breath background are accented by coral-to-pink helichrysum and several green leaves of myrtle. This corsage was chosen to contrast with a light turquoise dress, a fabric color that cannot be matched with flowers but can be attractively enhanced by compatible colors.

CARING FOR YOUR EVERLASTINGS

Once the everlasting arrangements have been used for the wedding ceremonies, people usually want some advice on how to preserve the flowers as long as possible. There are a few general rules about caring for everlastings. Dried materials should be protected from exposure to direct sunlight; otherwise the colors will quickly fade. Indirect natural light will not significantly diminish the brilliance of the colors and, depending on the flowers used, the colors should last for months and even years. Everlastings also suffer from prolonged exposure to humidity. Thus we often suggest that during the hot muggy days of summer in Maine, and whenever such weather occurs in other regions, one should wrap special wreaths or arrangements in tissue and store them in a box. Everlastings can be brought back out when the humidity level drops, usually in the early fall.

As for keeping the everlasting arrangements free of dust, we can offer no good advice beyond what our own common sense would suggest. A soft camel-hair brush can be used to dust off special flowers. A hair dryer, set to the lowest speed and held at some distance, will do a superficial job. Everlastings are sometimes erroneously believed to literally last forever. They will hold up for a very long time, but like any other natural fiber or color, they are subject to the chemistry of change. As arrangements gradually lose some of their initial brilliance and vibrancy, many of you will enjoy the slightly less colorful blending of tones, and in fact we have had a few designs that improved with the softening of hue. But you must decide for yourself when you want to part with the designs, or when you wish to refresh some of them with more recently grown material.

SOME TOOLS TO HAVE FOR WORK ON EVERLASTINGS

Throughout this chapter, we have referred to a few tools and materials that one should have on hand. We have grouped them into two photographs, one pertaining to general design and one more specifically to wedding arrangements. The tools are neither elaborate nor costly, and they are generally available from floral supply companies, individual florist shops or sometimes craft and hobby stores.

We will begin the descriptions in the top left-hand corner and continue around clockwise.

The gray brick of floral foam shown here is Sahara, but it is also manufactured under other trade names. You will most definitely want a supply of this for working in containers. The green floral foam typically used for fresh arrangements can be used in a pinch, but it will not hold together as well over a long time.

Next is one of a number of electric glue guns on the market. You will find this tool very useful for accenting and detailing work. The glue gun uses sticks of a wax-like glue that are available in varying lengths and colors. When the stick of glue heats up inside the gun, the glue is released by pulling the trigger. Although some designers would disagree, we resist the notion of gluing a whole project. The pleasure of working with real material comes from actually handling and respecting the shapes and forms of the material itself.

Crimped wire rings for making herbal wreaths come in a large variety of sizes. However, we have not yet found them smaller than 8″ in diameter, so we fashion our own for smaller wreaths.

You will, of course, need scissors for cutting

stems, ribbons and floral tape. You may also want to have a pair of wire cutters and heavy-duty garden stem cutters. The stems of larger materials, such as celosias, thick-stemmed grasses and the like, are a bit large for ordinary scissors.

Rolls of floral tape come in green and brown; we use both depending on the project.

Floral picks come in different sizes and lengths. You will use mostly the 2½" picks for wreath making, but various other lengths for arrangements.

Wire can be purchased in specific lengths or on rolls. The gauges also vary; specifics on wire gauges have been given in the preceding sections.

The heart-shaped crimped wire is simply a circle re-formed; you can fashion this on your own, rather than purchasing it.

The tools in this photograph are used primarily in making wedding arrangements. On the left are two different bouquet holders, one assembled and the other showing the two pieces. The handle with the floral foam attached is available in different sizes to match the size of the bouquet. The lace circle also comes in different sizes and in white and ivory. We usually cover the handles and backs of the lace holder with white or ivory fabric, since we feel that the cold plastic is both unsightly and unpleasing to the touch.

The pipe cleaners come in various colors and lengths, as do the hair combs.

You will want some boutonniere and corsage pins. They come in small boxes, with longer pins for the corsages, shorter ones for the boutonnieres.

As a final note about supplies, we suggest that you begin by purchasing small quantities of different materials and supplies. That will allow you to experiment with design ideas and techniques before making any large investment. As your work and experience increase, you will be better prepared to stock your workshop with the materials you most need and prefer, just as you will be able to plan your gardens and collecting for the designing you most enjoy.

Selected Bibliography

Anderson, Frank J. *Illustrated History of Herbals*. New York: Columbia University Press, 1977.

Anonymous. *The Sentiment of Flowers*. Philadelphia, 1840.

Bailey, L. H., et al. *Hortus Third*. New York: Macmillan, 1976.

Banerji, Sures Chandra. *Flora and Fauna in Sanskrit Literature*. Calcutta: Naya Prokash, 1980.

Beal, Dr. Alvin C. "Lectures on Gardening and the Use of Flowers." *Yearbook of the Horticultural Society of New York*, 1924.

Beals, Katharine M. *Flower Lore and Legend*. New York, 1917.

Bourne, Herman. *The Florist's Manual*. Boston: Munroe and Francis, 1833.

Breck, Joseph. *The Flower Garden*. Boston: Jewett, 1851.

Britton, Nathaniel L., and Addison Brown. *An Illustrated Flora of the Northern United States and Canada*. New York: Dover, 1970.

Brown, Lauren. *Grasses: An Identification Guide*. Boston: Houghton Mifflin, 1979.

Browne, Thomas. *Of Garlands and Coronary or Garland Plants to John Evelyn*. Northampton, 1962.

Coats, Alice M. *Flowers and Their Histories*. New York: McGraw-Hill, 1956.

De Waal Malefijt, Annemarie. *Images of Man*. New York: Knopf, 1974.

Embertson, Jane. *Pods*. New York: Scribner's, 1979.

Erichsen-Brown, Charlotte. *Use of Plants for the Past 500 Years*. Aurora, Canada: Breezy Creeks Press, 1984.

Fernald, Merritt. *Gray's Manual of Botany*. New York: Van Nostrand, 1970.

Folkard, Richard. *Plant Lore, Legends and Lyrics*. Sampson Low, 1884.

Friend, Hilderic. *Flowers and Flower Lore*. London, 1886. Reprint. Rockport, Maine: Para Research, Inc., 1981.

Gerard, John. *The Herbal*. New York: Dover, 1975 (orig. pub. 1633).

Gleason, Henry A. *Illustrated Flora of the Northeastern United States*. 3 vols. New York: New York Botanical Garden, 1952.

Hulme, Edward F. *History and Associations of Flowers*. London: Marcus Ward, 1877.

Johnson, Louisa. *Every Lady*. Charleston: S. Babcock, 1842.

Keese, John (ed.). *The Floral Keepsake*. New York: Leavitt, 1850.

Le Strange, Richard. *A History of Herbal Plants*. London: Angus and Robertson, 1977.

Madock, James. *The Florist's Directory*. London: The Author, 1792.

Millspaugh, Charles F. *American Medicinal Plants*. New York: Dover, 1974 (orig. pub. 1892).

Otten, Charlotte M. *Anthropology and Art*. Garden City, N.Y.: Natural History Press, 1971.

Powell, Claire. *The Meaning of Flowers*. Boulder: Shambhala, 1979.

Rees, Abraham. *Dictionary of Arts, Sciences and Literature*. London: Longman, Hurst, 1819.

Sargent, Frederick L. *The National Flower Movement*. Boston, 1899.

Saunders, Mary J. "The Flora of Colonial Days." *Bulletin of the Essex Institute*, 1895.

Smith, William. *Dictionary of Greek and Roman Biography and Mythology*. Boston: Little, Brown, 1859.

Solecki, Ralph S. "Shanidar IV, a Neanderthal Flower Burial in Northern Iraq." *Science*, November 28, 1975.

————. *Shanidar: The First Flower People*. New York: Knopf, 1971.

Steere, William C. (ed.). *Wild Flowers of the United States*. New York: McGraw-Hill–New York Botanical Garden, 1966.

Stuart, Malcolm. *Herbs and Herbalism*. New York: Van Nostrand, 1979.

Watkins, M. G. *Gleanings from the Natural History of the Ancients*. London: Elliot Stack, 1896.

Wood, Alphonso. *The New American Botanist and Florist*. New York: American Book Co., 1889.

Indexes

Family Index of Listed Species

PAGE NUMBER	FAMILY	GENUS	SPECIES	SUBSPECIES
88–89	Compositae	Cirsium	japonicum	
123	Compositae	Cirsium	vulgare	
89	Compositae	Coreopsis	lanceolata	
53–56	Compositae	Cotula	barbata	
91	Compositae	Echinops	ritro	
56	Compositae	Emilia	javanica	
124–125	Compositae	Eupatorium	perfoliatum	
125	Compositae	Eupatorium	purpureum	
91–92	Compositae	Gaillardia	× grandiflora	
125–128	Compositae	Gnaphalium	obtusifolium	
44, 57–58	Compositae	Helichrysum	bracteatum	monstrosum
57	Compositae	Helichrysum	orientale	
57	Compositae	Helichrysum	stoechas	
57	Compositae	Helichrysum	arenarium	
57	Compositae	Helichrysum	thianschanicum	
57	Compositae	Helichrysum	angustifolium	
58	Compositae	Helipterum	humboldtianum	
44, 58–59	Compositae	Helipterum	manglesii	
44, 59	Compositae	Helipterum	roseum	
128	Compositae	Hieracium	aurantiacum	
128	Compositae	Hieracium	villosum	
97	Compositae	Leontopodium	alpinum	
97	Compositae	Liatris	pycnostachya	
60	Compositae	Lonas	annua	
62–63	Compositae	Ratibida	columnifera	
107–108	Compositae	Rudbeckia	hirta	
109–110	Compositae	Santolina	chamaecyparissus	
64	Compositae	Scabiosa	stellata	
140	Compositae	Solidago	canadensis	and spp.
64–65	Compositae	Tagetes	erecta	
110–111	Compositae	Tanacetum	vulgare	
43, 65	Compositae	Xeranthemum	annuum	
110	Crassulaceae	Sedum	spectabile	
122	Cruciferae	Capsella	bursa-pastoris	
129	Cruciferae	Lepidium	campestre	
99	Cruciferae	Lunaria	annua	
129	Cruciferae	Thlaspi	arvense	
122	Cyperaceae	Carex	lurida	
122	Cyperaceae	Eriophorum	virginicum	
90–91	Dipsacaceae	Dipsacus	fullonum	
84	Ericaceae	Calluna	vulgaris	
47	Gramineae	Agrostis	spp.	
47	Gramineae	Avena	sterilis	
47	Gramineae	Briza	maxima	
47	Gramineae	Coix	lacryma	jobi
89–90	Gramineae	Cortaderia	selloana	
47	Gramineae	Eragrostis	spp.	
130–136	Gramineae	Phragmites	australis	
47	Gramineae	Secale	spp.	
47	Gramineae	Setaria	spp.	
89–90	Gramineae	Stipa	pennata	
89–90	Gramineae	Stipa	avenacea	
47	Gramineae	Triticum	spp.	
128	Iridaceae	Iris	versicolor	
128–129	Juncaceae	Juncus	canadensis	and spp.
94–96	Labiatae	Hyssopus	officinale	
96–97	Labiatae	Lavandula	angustifolia	
100	Labiatae	Mentha	spicata	
60–61	Labiatae	Moluccella	laevis	
100–102	Labiatae	Monarda	fistulosa	

PAGE NUMBER	FAMILY	GENUS	SPECIES	SUBSPECIES
102	Labiatae	Nepeta	mussinii	
62	Labiatae	Ocimum	basilicum	
62	Labiatae	Ocimum	kilimandjaricum	
62	Labiatae	Ocimum	sanctum	
102	Labiatae	Origanum	majorana	
102	Labiatae	Origanum	vulgare	
106	Labiatae	Physostegia	virginiana	
106–107	Labiatae	Pycnanthemum	incanum	
43, 63	Labiatae	Salvia	farinaceae	
43, 63–64	Labiatae	Salvia	splendens	
64	Labiatae	Salvia	viridis	
108–109	Labiatae	Salvia	officinalis	
109	Labiatae	Salvia	× superba	
110	Labiatae	Stachys	byzantina	
123	Leguminosae	Coronilla	varia	
141	Leguminosae	Trifolium	agrarium	
141	Leguminosae	Trifolium	arvense	
141	Leguminosae	Vicia	cracca	
130	Lythraceae	Lythrum	salicaria	
44	Malvaceae	Abutilon	theophrasti	
99–100	Malvaceae	Malva	moschata	
56	Myrtaceae	Eucalyptus	cinerea	
124	Onagranaceae	Epilobium	angustifolium	
103	Papaveraceae	Papaver	orientale	
136	Plantaginaceae	Plantago	major	
77–80	Plumbaginaceae	Armeria	maritima	
92	Plumbaginaceae	Goniolimon	tataricum	
44, 59–60	Plumbaginaceae	Limonium	bonduellii	
44, 59–60	Plumbaginaceae	Limonium	sinuatum	
97–99	Plumbaginaceae	Limonium	latifolium	
129–130	Plumbaginaceae	Limonium	nashii	
62	Plumbaginaceae	Psylliostachys	suworowii	
136–137	Polygonaceae	Polygonella	articulata	
137	Polygonaceae	Polygonum	orientale	
138	Polygonaceae	Rumex	acetosa	
77	Ranunculaceae	Aquilegia	× hybrida	
88	Ranunculaceae	Cimicifuga	racemosa	
123	Ranunculaceae	Clematis	virginiana	
53	Ranunculaceae	Consolida	ambigua	
90	Ranunculaceae	Delphinium	× cultorum	
61–62	Ranunculaccac	Nigella	damascena	
74	Rosaceae	Alchemilla	vulgaris	
137	Rosaceae	Potentilla	arguta	
106	Rosaceae	Poterium	sanguisorba	
107	Rosaceae	Rosa	spp.	
140–141	Rosaceae	Spiraea	tomentosa	
122–123	Rubiaceae	Cephalanthus	occidentalis	
108	Rutaceae	Ruta	graveolens	
48	Sapindaceae	Cardiospermum	halicacabum	
84	Saxifragaceae	Astilbe	× arendsii	
94	Saxifragaceae	Heuchera	sanguinea	
94	Saxifragaceae	Hydrangea	paniculata	
130	Scrophulariaceae	Linaria	vulgaris	
111	Scrophulariaceae	Veronica	spicata	
61	Solanaceae	Nicandra	physalodes	
103	Solanaceae	Physalis	alkekengi	
136	Solanaceae	Physalis	heterophylla	
124	Umbelliferae	Daucus	carota	
91	Umbelliferae	Eryngium	planum	
141	Verbenaceae	Verbena	hastata	

Genus Index of Listed Species

Common Name Index

PAGE NUMBER	COMMON NAME	GENUS	SPECIES	SUBSPECIES
80–81	absinthe	Artemisia	absinthium	
106	accommodation flower	Physostegia	virginiana	
44, 59	acroclinium	Helipterum	roseum	
124	adder's wort	Echium	vulgare	
44–45	ageratum	Ageratum	houstonianum	
24–125	ague-weed	Eupatorium	perfoliatum	
94	alumroot	Heuchera	sanguinea	
45–46	amaranthus	Amaranthus	caudatus	
52	ambrosia	Chenopodium	botrys	
43, 46	ammobium	Ammobium	alatum	grandiflora
47	animated oats	Avena	sterilis	
53	annual delphinium	Consolida	ambigua	
46	annual wormwood	Artemisia	annua	
61	apple-of-Peru	Nicandra	physalodes	
84	astilbe	Astilbe	×arendsii	
123	axseed	Coronilla	varia	
123	axwort	Coronilla	varia	
92	baby's breath	Gypsophila	paniculata	
49–52	bachelor's button	Centaurea	cyanus	
48	balloon vine	Cardiospermum	halicacabum	
125–128	balsam weed	Gnaphalium	obtusifolium	
110	band-aid plant	Stachys	byzantina	
123	bank thistle	Cirsium	vulgare	
62	basil	Ocimum	basilicum	
129	bastard cress	Lepidium	campestre	
48–49	bastard saffron	Carthamus	tinctorius	
119	beach wormwood	Artemisia	stelleriana	
100–102	bee balm	Monarda	fistulosa	
123	bell-thistle	Cirsium	vulgare	
60–61	bells of Ireland	Moluccella	laevis	
130–136	bennels	Phragmites	australis	
124	bird's nest plant	Daucus	carota	
137	biting knotweed	Polygonum	orientale	
87	bittersweet	Celastrus	scandens	
88	black cohosh	Cimicifuga	racemosa	
89–90	black oat-grass	Stipa	avenacea	
88	black snakeroot	Cimicifuga	racemosa	
107–108	black-eyed Susan	Rudbeckia	hirta	
103	bladder cherry	Physalis	alkekengi	
91–92	blanket flower	Gaillardia	×grandiflora	
97	blazing-star	Liatris	pycnostachya	
72–73	bloodwort	Achillea	millefolium	
128	blue flag	Iris	versicolor	
43, 63	blue salvia	Salvia	farinacea	Victoria, Catima
124	blue stem	Echium	vulgare	
124	blue thistle	Echium	vulgare	
141	blue vervain	Verbena	hastata	
141	blue vetch	Vicia	cracca	
49–52	blue-bottle	Centaurea	cyanus	
124	blue-devil	Echium	vulgare	
124	blueweed	Echium	vulgare	
123	boar thistle	Cirsium	vulgare	
99	bolbonac	Lunaria	annua	
124–125	boneset	Eupatorium	perfoliatum	
141	bottle grass	Trifolium	arvense	
138	bouncing Bet	Saponaria	officinalis	
122–123	box	Cephalanthus	occidentalis	
130	bread-and-butter	Linaria	vulgaris	
130	brideweed	Linaria	vulgaris	
111	brooklime	Veronica	spicata	

PAGE NUMBER	COMMON NAME	GENUS	SPECIES	SUBSPECIES
123	devil's hair	Clematis	virginiana	
128	devil's paintbrush	Hieracium	aurantiacum	
124	devil's plague	Daucus	carota	
97	devilsbit	Liatris	pycnostachya	
47	dithering grass	Briza	maxima	
47	dodder grass	Briza	maxima	
141	dogs-and-cats	Trifolium	arvense	
110	donkey ear	Stachys	byzantina	
136	dooryard plantain	Plantago	major	
119	dusty miller	Artemisia	stelleriana	
52–53	dusty miller	Chrysanthemum	ptarmiciflorum	
57	dwarf yellow immortelle	Helichrysum	arenarium	
97	edelweiss	Leontopodium	alpinum	
130	eggs-and-bacon	Linaria	vulgaris	
56	eucalyptus	Eucalyptus	cinerea	
44, 57–58	everlasting	Helichrysum	bracteatum	monstrosum
47	fairy grass	Briza	maxima	
87	false bittersweet	Celastrus	scandens	
106	false dragonhead	Physostegia	virginiana	
129	false flax	Lepidium	campestre	
84	false goatsbeard	Astilbe	×arendsii	
48–49	false saffron	Carthamus	tinctorius	
141	false vervain	Verbena	hastata	
47	feather grass	Stipa	spp.	
125–128	feather weed	Gnaphalium	obtusifolium	
52	feather-geranium	Chenopodium	botrys	
82	felon herb	Artemisia	vulgaris	
72	fern-leafy yarrow	Achillea	filipendulina	
87–88	feverfew	Chrysanthemum	parthenium	
124–125	feverwort	Eupatorium	perfoliatum	
129	field cress	Lepidium	campestre	
129	field pennycress	Thlaspi	arvense	
124	fireweed	Epilobium	angustifolium	
128	flag lily	Iris	versicolor	
130	flaxweed	Linaria	vulgaris	
49	floramor	Celosia	argentea	
44–45	floss flower	Ageratum	houstonianum	
140	flower of gold	Solidago	canadensis	
49	flower velure	Celosia	argentea	
128	flower-de-luce	Iris	versicolor	
47	foxtail millet	Setaria	spp.	
125–128	fragrant everlasting	Gnaphalium	obtusifolium	
110	frog's belly	Sedum	spectabile	
125–128	fussy gussy	Gnaphalium	obtusifolium	
130	gallwort	Linaria	vulgaris	
77	garden crowfoot	Aquilegia	×hybrida	
74–76	garlic chive	Allium	tuberosum	
97	gay-feather	Liatris	pycnostachya	
129	glen pepper	Lepidium	campestre	
44, 56–57	globe amaranth	Gomphrena	globosa	
87	globe centaurea	Centaurea	macrocephala	
122–123	globe flower	Cephalanthus	occidentalis	
91	globe thistle	Echinops	ritro	
107–108	gloriosa daisy	Rudbeckia	hirta	
60	golden ageratum	Lonas	annua	
57	golden baby	Helichrysum	angustifolium	
57	golden Cassidony	Helichrysum	stoechas	
87–88	golden feverfew	Chrysanthemum	parthenium	eximia
57	golden mothwort	Helichrysum	orientale	
128	golden mouse-ear hawkweed	Hieracium	aurantiacum	

PAGE NUMBER	COMMON NAME	GENUS	SPECIES	SUBSPECIES
128–129	rush	Juncus	spp.	
47	rye	Secale	spp.	
48–49	safflower	Carthamus	tinctorius	
108–109	sage	Salvia	officinalis	
130	sage-willow	Lythrum	salicaria	
122	sallow sedge	Carex	lurida	
43	salvia	Salvia	splendens	
64	salvia	Salvia	viridis	
109	salvia	Salvia	×superba	
136–137	sand knotweed	Polygonella	articulata	
72–73	sanguinary	Achillea	millefolium	
99	satin flower	Lunaria	annua	
110	saviour's blanket	Stachys	byzantina	
64	scabiosa	Scabiosa	stellata	
43, 63–64	scarlet sage	Salvia	splendens	
91	sea holly	Eryngium	planum	
97–99	sea lavender	Limonium	latifolium	
129–130	sea lavender	Limonium	nashii	
77–80	sea pink	Armeria	maritima	
122	sedge	Carex	lurida	
138	sharp dock	Rumex	acetosa	
138	sheep sorrel	Rumex	acetosa	
44	sheep weed	Abutilon	theophrasti	
138	sheepweed	Saponaria	officinalis	
60–61	shellflower	Moluccella	laevis	
122	shepherd's purse	Capsella	bursa-pastoris	
73–74	shirtbuttons	Achillea	ptarmica	
61	shoo-fly plant	Nicandra	physalodes	
122	shovel-weed	Capsella	bursa-pastoris	
119	silkweed	Asclepias	syriaca	
76–77	silver button	Anaphalis	margaritacea	
81	Silver King	Artemisia	ludoviciana	
52–53	silver lace	Chrysanthemum	ptarmiciflorum	
82	Silver Mound	Artemisia	schmidtiana	nana
81	Silver Queen	Artemisia	ludoviciana	albula
99	silver-dollar	Lunaria	annua	
76–77	silver-leaf	Anaphalis	margaritacea	
140–141	silver-leaf	Spiraea	tomentosa	
138–140	sleepy catchfly	Silene	antirrhina	
137	smartweed	Polygonum	orientale	
124	snake flower	Echium	vulgare	
128	snake liver	Iris	versicolor	
73–74	sneezeweed	Achillea	ptarmica	
73–74	sneezewort	Achillea	ptarmica	
122–123	snowball	Cephalanthus	occidentalis	
138	soap root	Saponaria	officinalis	
138	soapwort	Saponaria	officinalis	
72–73	soldier's woundwort	Achillea	millefolium	
130	soldiers	Lythrum	salicaria	
138	sorrel	Rumex	acetosa	
138	sour sorrel	Rumex	acetosa	
80–81	southernwood	Artemisia	abrotanum	
123	spear thistle	Cirsium	vulgare	
100	spearmint	Mentha	spicata	
111	speedwell	Veronica	spicata	
140–141	spice-hardhack	Spiraea	tomentosa	
130	spiked willow-herb	Lythrum	salicaria	
130–136	spires	Phragmites	australis	
87	staff vine	Celastrus	scandens	
137–138	staghorn sumac	Rhus	typhina	

Botanical Name Index

PAGE NUMBER	GENUS	SPECIES	SUBSPECIES	COMMON NAME
73–74	Achillea	ptarmica		sneezeweed
73–74	Achillea	ptarmica		sneezewort
73–74	Achillea	ptarmica		the pearl
72	Achillea	filipendulina		fern-leafy yarrow
72	Achillea	filipendulina		golden yarrow
72	Achillea	filipendulina		yellow yarrow
74	Achillea	tomentosa	aurea	woolly yarrow
44–45	Ageratum	houstonianum		ageratum
44–45	Ageratum	houstonianum		floss flower
44–45	Ageratum	houstonianum		pussy-foot
47	Agrostis	spp.		cloud grass
74	Alchemilla	vulgaris		lady's mantle
74	Alchemilla	vulgaris		lion's foot
74–76	Allium	ampeloprasum		leek
74–76	Allium	cepa		onion
74–76	Allium	schoenoprasum		chive
74–76	Allium	tuberosum		garlic chive
45–46	Amaranthus	caudatus		love-lies-bleeding
45–46	Amaranthus	caudatus		tassel flower
45–46	Amaranthus	hybridus		pigweed
45–46	Amaranthus	hypochondriacus	erythrostachys	prince's feather
45–46	Amaranthus	tricolor		Joseph's coat
45–46	Amaranthus	tricolor		tampala
46	Ammobium	alatum	grandiflora	winged everlasting
76–77	Anaphalis	margaritacea		Indian posy
76–77	Anaphalis	margaritacea		cad-weed
76–77	Anaphalis	margaritacea		cotton weed
76–77	Anaphalis	margaritacea		ladies' tobacco
76–77	Anaphalis	margaritacea		life everlasting
76–77	Anaphalis	margaritacea		moonshine
76–77	Anaphalis	margaritacea		none so pretty
76–77	Anaphalis	margaritacea		pearly everlasting
76–77	Anaphalis	margaritacea		rabbit-tobacco
76–77	Anaphalis	margaritacea		silver button
76–77	Anaphalis	margaritacea		silver-leaf
119	Antennaria	neglecta		cat's foot
119	Antennaria	neglecta		cudweed
119	Antennaria	neglecta		ladies' tobacco
119	Antennaria	neglecta		life everlasting
119	Antennaria	neglecta		pussy-toes
77	Aquilegia	× hybrida		European crowfoot
77	Aquilegia	× hybrida		columbine
77	Aquilegia	× hybrida		garden crowfoot
77–80	Armeria	maritima		ladies' cushion
77–80	Armeria	maritima		sea pink
77–80	Armeria	maritima		thrift
80–81	Artemisia	absinthium		absinthe
80–81	Artemisia	absinthium		ware-moth
80–81	Artemisia	absinthium		wormwood
82	Artemisia	schmidtiana	nana	Silver Mound
119	Artemisia	stelleriana		beach wormwood
119	Artemisia	stelleriana		dusty miller
80–81	Artemisia	abrotanum		southernwood
46	Artemisia	annua		annual wormwood
46	Artemisia	annua		sweet wormwood
80–81	Artemisia	drucunculus		Russian tarragon
80–81	Artemisia	drucunculus	sativa	French tarragon
81	Artemisia	ludoviciana		Silver King
81	Artemisia	ludoviciana	albula	Silver Queen
81–82	Artemisia	pontica		Roman wormwood

PAGE NUMBER	GENUS	SPECIES	SUBSPECIES	COMMON NAME
53	Consolida	ambigua		annual delphinium
53	Consolida	ambigua		knight's spur
53	Consolida	ambigua		lark's toe
53	Consolida	ambigua		larkspur
89	Coreopsis	lanceolata		tickseed
123	Coronilla	varia		axseed
123	Coronilla	varia		axwort
123	Coronilla	varia		crown vetch
123	Coronilla	varia		hive-vine
89–90	Cortaderia	selloana		pampas grass
53–56	Cotula	barbata		pincushion plant
124	Daucus	carota		bird's nest plant
124	Daucus	carota		crow's nest
124	Daucus	carota		devil's plague
124	Daucus	carota		lace flower
124	Daucus	carota		parsnip
124	Daucus	carota		Queen Anne's lace
124	Daucus	carota		rantipole
90	Delphinium	×cultorum		delphinium
90–91	Dipsacus	fullonum		teasel
91	Echinops	ritro		globe thistle
124	Echium	vulgare		adder's wort
124	Echium	vulgare		blue stem
124	Echium	vulgare		blue thistle
124	Echium	vulgare		blue-devil
124	Echium	vulgare		blueweed
124	Echium	vulgare		cat's tail
124	Echium	vulgare		snake flower
124	Echium	vulgare		viper's bugloss
124	Echium	vulgare		viper's grass
124	Echium	vulgare		viper's herb
56	Emilia	javanica		Cacalia coccinea
56	Emilia	javanica		Emilia sagittata
56	Emilia	javanica		Flora's paintbrush
56	Emilia	javanica		tassel flower
124	Epilobium	angustifolium		wickup
124	Epilobium	angustifolium		fireweed
124	Epilobium	angustifolium		great willow herb
124	Epilobium	angustifolium		wickopy
124	Epilobium	angustifolium		widkiup
47	Eragrostis	spp.		love grass
122	Eriophorum	virginicum		cotton grass
91	Eryngium	alpinum		sea holly
56	Eucalyptus	cinerea		eucalyptus
124–125	Eupatorium	perfoliatum		Indian sage
124–125	Eupatorium	perfoliatum		ague-weed
124–125	Eupatorium	perfoliatum		boneset
124–125	Eupatorium	perfoliatum		common thoroughwort
124–125	Eupatorium	perfoliatum		crosswort
124–125	Eupatorium	perfoliatum		feverwort
124–125	Eupatorium	perfoliatum		sweating weed
124–125	Eupatorium	perfoliatum		thorough wax
124–125	Eupatorium	perfoliatum		vegetable antimony
125	Eupatorium	purpureum		Joe-Pye weed
125	Eupatorium	purpureum		Jopi weed
125	Eupatorium	purpureum		gravel root
125	Eupatorium	purpureum		hemp-weed
125	Eupatorium	purpureum		purple boneset
125	Eupatorium	purpureum		queen of the meadow
125	Eupatorium	purpureum		thoroughwort

PAGE NUMBER	GENUS	SPECIES	SUBSPECIES	COMMON NAME
129	Lepidium	campestre		Mithridate mustard
129	Lepidium	campestre		bastard cress
129	Lepidium	campestre		cow cress
129	Lepidium	campestre		crowd weed
129	Lepidium	campestre		false flax
129	Lepidium	campestre		field cress
129	Lepidium	campestre		glen pepper
129	Lepidium	campestre		poor-man's pepper
129	Lepidium	campestre		yellow seed
97	Liatris	pycnostachya		blazing-star
97	Liatris	pycnostachya		button-snakeroot
97	Liatris	pycnostachya		colic-root
97	Liatris	pycnostachya		devilsbit
97	Liatris	pycnostachya		gay-feather
97	Liatris	pycnostachya		rattlesnake master
44, 59–60	Limonium	bonduellii		statice
97–99	Limonium	latifolium		marsh rosemary
97–99	Limonium	latifolium		sea lavender
129–130	Limonium	nashii		American thrift
129–130	Limonium	nashii		canker root
129–130	Limonium	nashii		ink root
129–130	Limonium	nashii		lavender thrift
129–130	Limonium	nashii		marsh rosemary
129–130	Limonium	nashii		sea lavender
44, 59–60	Limonium	sinuatum		leadwort
44, 59–60	Limonium	sinuatum		marsh rosemary
44, 59–60	Limonium	sinuatum		statice
130	Linaria	vulgaris		Jacob's ladder
130	Linaria	vulgaris		bread-and-butter
130	Linaria	vulgaris		brideweed
130	Linaria	vulgaris		butter-and-eggs
130	Linaria	vulgaris		common toadflax
130	Linaria	vulgaris		continental weed
130	Linaria	vulgaris		dead men's bones
130	Linaria	vulgaris		devil's flax
130	Linaria	vulgaris		devil's flower
130	Linaria	vulgaris		eggs-and-bacon
130	Linaria	vulgaris		flaxweed
130	Linaria	vulgaris		gallwort
130	Linaria	vulgaris		impudent lawyer
130	Linaria	vulgaris		rabbit-flower
130	Linaria	vulgaris		rancid
130	Linaria	vulgaris		ranstead
130	Linaria	vulgaris		wild snapdragon
130	Linaria	vulgaris		wild tobacco
130	Linaria	vulgaris		yellow toadflax
60	Lonas	annua		African daisy
60	Lonas	annua		Lonas inodora
60	Lonas	annua		golden ageratum
60	Lonas	annua		yellow ageratum
99	Lunaria	annua		Lunaria biennis
99	Lunaria	annua		bolbonac
99	Lunaria	annua		honest pocketbook
99	Lunaria	annua		honesty
99	Lunaria	annua		money plant
99	Lunaria	annua		money-in-both-pockets
99	Lunaria	annua		moon-penny
99	Lunaria	annua		moonwort
99	Lunaria	annua		satin flower
99	Lunaria	annua		silver-dollar

PAGE NUMBER	GENUS	SPECIES	SUBSPECIES	COMMON NAME
130	Lythrum	salicaria		kill-weed
130	Lythrum	salicaria		long purples
130	Lythrum	salicaria		purple loosestrife
130	Lythrum	salicaria		purple-grass
130	Lythrum	salicaria		rainbow weed
130	Lythrum	salicaria		red Sally
130	Lythrum	salicaria		sage-willow
130	Lythrum	salicaria		soldiers
130	Lythrum	salicaria		spiked willow-herb
130	Lythrum	salicaria		willow weed
99–100	Malva	moschata		mallow
99–100	Malva	moschata		musk mallow
100	Mentha	spicata		spearmint
60–61	Moluccella	laevis		Molucca balm
60–61	Moluccella	laevis		bells of Ireland
60–61	Moluccella	laevis		shellflower
100–102	Monarda	fistulosa		Oswego Tea
100–102	Monarda	fistulosa		bee balm
100–102	Monarda	fistulosa		horsemint
100–102	Monarda	fistulosa		wild bergamot
102	Nepeta	mussinii		catmint
61	Nicandra	physalodes		nicandra
61	Nicandra	physalodes		apple-of-Peru
61	Nicandra	physalodes		shoo-fly plant
61–62	Nigella	damascena		nigella
61–62	Nigella	damascena		love-in-a-puzzle
61–62	Nigella	damascena		love-in-the-mist
61–62	Nigella	damascena		wild fennel
62	Ocimum	basilicum		basil
62	Ocimum	kilimandjaricum		camphor basil
62	Ocimum	sanctum		holy basil
102	Origanum	majorana		sweet marjoram
102	Origanum	vulgare		oregano
103	Papaver	orientale		Oriental poppy
130–136	Phragmites	australis		common reed
130–136	Phragmites	australis		Dutch reed
130–136	Phragmites	australis		bennels
130–136	Phragmites	australis		pole reed
130–136	Phragmites	australis		reed
130–136	Phragmites	australis		spires
130–136	Phragmites	australis		wild broom corn
103	Physalis	alkekengi		Chinese lantern
103	Physalis	alkekengi		Japanese lantern
103	Physalis	alkekengi		Physalis Franchetii
103	Physalis	alkekengi		bladder cherry
103	Physalis	alkekengi		strawberry tomato
103	Physalis	alkekengi		winter cherry
136	Physalis	heterophylla		clammy ground cherry
136	Physalis	heterophylla		ground cherry
106	Physostegia	virginiana		American heather
106	Physostegia	virginiana		Mexican heath
106	Physostegia	virginiana		false dragonhead
106	Physostegia	virginiana		obedient plant
106	Physostegia	virginiana		accommodation flower
136	Plantago	major		dooryard plantain
136	Plantago	major		healing-blade
136	Plantago	major		hen-plant
136	Plantago	major		lamb's foot
136	Plantago	major		plantain
136	Plantago	major		rib-grass

PAGE NUMBER	GENUS	SPECIES	SUBSPECIES	COMMON NAME
136	Plantago	major		rib-wort
136	Plantago	major		round-leaf plantain
136	Plantago	major		way-bread
136–137	Polygonella	articulata		coast jointweed
136–137	Polygonella	articulata		coast knotweed
136–137	Polygonella	articulata		sand knotweed
136–137	Polygonella	articulata		jointed knotweed
137	Polygonum	orientale		biting knotweed
137	Polygonum	orientale		kiss-me-over-garden-gate
137	Polygonum	orientale		prince's feather
137	Polygonum	orientale		princess feather
137	Polygonum	orientale		smartweed
137	Polygonum	orientale		water pepper
137	Potentilla	arguta		cinquefoil
137	Potentilla	arguta		tall cinquefoil
106	Poterium	sanguisorba		burnet
62	Psylliostachys	suworowii		Limonium Suworowii
62	Psylliostachys	suworowii		Russian statice
62	Psylliostachys	suworowii		rat-tail statice
106–107	Pycnanthemum	incanum		hoary mountain mint
106–107	Pycnanthemum	incanum		mountain mint
62–63	Ratibida	columnifera		Mexican hat plant
62–63	Ratibida	columnifera		prairie coneflower
137–138	Rhus	typhina		American sumac
137–138	Rhus	typhina		Virginia sumac
137–138	Rhus	typhina		hairy sumac
137–138	Rhus	typhina		staghorn sumac
137–138	Rhus	typhina		velvet sumac
137–138	Rhus	typhina		vinegar tree
107	Rosa	spp.		rose
107–108	Rudbeckia	hirta		black-eyed Susan
107–108	Rudbeckia	hirta		gloriosa daisy
138	Rumex	acetosa		green sorrel
138	Rumex	acetosa		sharp dock
138	Rumex	acetosa		sheep sorrel
138	Rumex	acetosa		sour sorrel
138	Rumex	acetosa		sorrel
108	Ruta	graveolens		rue, herb-of-grace
43, 63	Salvia	farinacea	Victoria, Catima	blue salvia
43, 63	Salvia	farinacea	Victoria, Catima	mealy-cup sage
108–109	Salvia	officinalis		sage
43, 63–64	Salvia	splendens		scarlet sage
64	Salvia	viridis		Salvia horminum
64	Salvia	viridis		salvia
109	Salvia	×superba	Blue and Rose Queen	salvia
109–110	Santolina	chamaecyparissus		French lavender
109–110	Santolina	chamaecyparissus		lavender cotton
138	Saponaria	officinalis		Boston pink
138	Saponaria	officinalis		Fuller's herb
138	Saponaria	officinalis		London pride
138	Saponaria	officinalis		bouncing Bet
138	Saponaria	officinalis		bruise-wort
138	Saponaria	officinalis		chimney pink
138	Saponaria	officinalis		lady-by-the-gate
138	Saponaria	officinalis		mock-gilliflower
138	Saponaria	officinalis		old-maid's pink
138	Saponaria	officinalis		sheepweed
138	Saponaria	officinalis		soap root
138	Saponaria	officinalis		soapwort

PAGE NUMBER	GENUS	SPECIES	SUBSPECIES	COMMON NAME
138	Saponaria	officinalis		sweet Betty
138	Saponaria	officinalis		wild Sweet William
138	Saponaria	officinalis		wood's phlox
138	Saponaria	officinalis		world's wonder
64	Scabiosa	stellata		paper moon
64	Scabiosa	stellata		star flower
64	Scabiosa	stellata		scabiosa
47	Secale	spp.		rye
110	Sedum	spectabile		frog's belly
110	Sedum	spectabile		live-forever
110	Sedum	spectabile		orpine
110	Sedum	spectabile		stone crop
47	Setaria	spp.		foxtail millet
138–140	Silene	antirrhina		sleepy catchfly
140	Solidago	canadensis		flower of gold
140	Solidago	canadensis		rock goldenrod
140	Solidago	canadensis		yellow top
140	Solidago	canadensis		yellow weed
140	Solidago	canadensis	and other spp.	goldenrod
140–141	Spiraea	tomentosa		hardhack
140–141	Spiraea	tomentsoa		meadow-sweet
140–141	Spiraea	tomentosa		poor man's soap
140–141	Spiraea	tomentosa		rosy-bush
140–141	Spiraea	tomentosa		silver-leaf
140–141	Spiraea	tomentosa		spice-hardhack
140–141	Spiraea	tomentosa		steeplebush
140–141	Spiraca	tomentosa		white cap
110	Stachys	byzantina		donkey ear
110	Stachys	byzantina		Stachys lanata
110	Stachys	byzantina		band-aid plant
110	Stachys	byzantina		lamb's tongue
110	Stachys	byzantina		lamb's ears
110	Stachys	hyzantina		mouse's ear
110	Stachys	byzantina		saviour's blanket
47	Stipa	spp.		feather grass
89–90	Stipa	avenacea		black oat-grass
89–90	Stipa	pennata		European feather grass
64–65	Tagetes	erecta		African marigold
64–65	Tagetes	erecta		Aztec marigold
64–65	Tagetes	erecta		marigold
110–111	Tanacetum	vulgare		golden-buttons
110–111	Tanacetum	vulgare		tansy
129	Thlaspi	arvense		field pennycress
141	Trifolium	agrarium		hop clover
141	Trifolium	arvense		bottle grass
141	Trifolium	arvense		dogs-and-cats
141	Trifolium	arvense		poverty grass
141	Trifolium	arvense		pussies
141	Trifolium	arvense		pussy-cats
141	Trifolium	arvense		rabbit-foot clover
47	Triticum	spp.		wheat
141	Verbena	hastata		American vervain
141	Verbena	hastata		blue vervain
141	Verbena	hastata		false vervain
141	Verbena	hastata		iron-weed
141	Verbena	hastata		purvain
141	Verbena	hastata		wild hyssop
111	Veronica	spicata		brooklime
111	Veronica	spicata		speedwell
141	Vicia	cracca		Canada peas

Botanical Name Index

PAGE NUMBER	GENUS	SPECIES	SUBSPECIES	COMMON NAME
141	Vicia	cracca		blue vetch
141	Vicia	cracca		cat peas
141	Vicia	cracca		cow vetch
141	Vicia	cracca		tinegrass
141	Vicia	cracca		tufted vetch
141	Vicia	cracca		vetch
111–112	Vinca	major		myrtle
111–112	Vinca	major		periwinkle
43, 65	Xeranthemum	annuum		immortelle

A NOTE ABOUT THE AUTHORS

Mark and Terry Silber are gardeners and co-founders/owners of
Hedgehog Hill Farm, in Sumner, Maine. In addition, Mark does
consulting and research for various agencies, and Terry is a design
consultant for Boston-based publishing companies. Mark took his A.B.
in biology from Harvard and his M.A. and Ph.D. from Boston
University in medical anthropology. He has taught at Garland Junior
College and at Boston University and has worked as a freelance
photojournalist, editor, writer, and designer. He is the author of *Rural
Maine* and *Racing Stock*, and editor of *Family Album* and *Thoreau Country*.
He has had photographic exhibitions at Addison Gallery of American
Art, Columbus Museum of Arts, Phoenix Museum of Arts, and
Birmingham Museum of Art. Terry Silber took her A.B. in French at
the University of New Hampshire and did graduate work in philosophy
at the University of Colorado and language study at Harvard. She has
taught French, been on the staffs of the Smithsonian Astrophysical
Observatory and the New England Regional Primate Research Center,
and done freelance design and writing. From 1970 to 1978 she
was art director for the *Atlantic Monthly*. She is the author of *A Small
Farm in Maine*.